Journeying in the Wilderness

Journeying in the Wilderness

Forming Faith in the 21st Century

Terri Martinson Elton

Fortress Press
Minneapolis

JOURNEYING IN THE WILDERNESS
Forming Faith in the 21st Century

Cover image: This Is The Way, Walk In It by Yuin Lu Hoo. iStock © 2019.
Cover design: Alisha Lofgren
Typesetting: PerfecType, Nashville, TN

Print ISBN: 978-1-5064-5560-0
eBook ISBN: 978-1-5064-5561-7

To my parents—Roland and Sharon Martinson

CONTENTS

Introduction

I remember that morning well: I was seven years old, sleeping in my second-floor bedroom, and woke to the house shaking. As my eyes focused, I noticed the pictures on the wall were crooked. Before I could say anything, the door opened, and my mom appeared. She carried me down the stairs as the house shook again. We headed to my parents' bedroom, where Mom placed me in bed with the rest of the family. As the shaking stopped, I learned we had lived through our first earthquake. With a magnitude of 6.6, it was the fourth largest in Glendale, California's history.[1]

The earthquake hit at 6:00 a.m. as Los Angeles was coming to life. There were fifty-eight casualties at a nearby hospital and nursing home; however, there could have been more if not for the early hour. Buildings were hit the hardest. Thousands of homes, schools, businesses, and churches experienced structural damage. Some damage was visible; some was not. It would take time to determine which structures were trustworthy and which needed repair. Yet buildings were not all that was shaken.

The days that followed were eerie. In the next few weeks, over two hundred aftershocks rocked the area, four with a magnitude of 5.0 or above.[2] They were unpredictable and disruptive. While I was at school or playing in the yard, the earth would suddenly shake, catching me off guard and making it hard to balance. Soon I began to question something as foundational as the ground.

Every day, we make assumptions about the foundations of our lives. When these assumptions get disrupted, it's hard to get our bearings. Disruptions disorient and make us feel out of control. Living through an earthquake was the first of many disruptions I would experience. In five decades, I have endured seismic shifts in almost every area of life. Some shifts were gradual, giving me time to adapt; others were abrupt, requiring an immediate response. Disruptions are now challenging assumptions in all aspects of life.

Present-day leaders wonder about the stability of the ground on which they stand. Their concern has merit. Forces are challenging our assumptions, commitments, and patterns of life. These forces are more than the winds of change or birth pains of progress; they are altering our way of life. Their impact is felt across organizations, disciplines, domains, and cultures. We cannot ignore them, and we do not want to be paralyzed by them. Moving forward requires finding our way through them.

Living in California for six years, I eventually learned to distinguish between major earthquakes and minor tremors. This recalibration allowed me to regain trust in fundamental beliefs and navigate daily life. Disruptions require recalibration, so recalibrating has become part of twenty-first-century living. Consciously or unconsciously, everyday life is forcing us to reimagine communication patterns, rethink values, discover new habits, and reflect on relationships. As we recalibrate life, what is the role of faith and faith communities?

Recalibrating Faith Formation

Listening to the church, I wonder how congregational practices align with people's everyday realities. Do pastors know people's heartfelt questions? Are our congregational gatherings addressing the challenges people encounter at home or work? Does the church offer a vision expansive enough for living abundantly in a consumer-driven, digitally mediated, socially networked, globally connected, religiously pluralistic world? I fear the answer is no.

Listening to the questions and concerns of young adults has challenged me to reflect on my assumptions and previous approaches to forming faith. The church's goals (i.e., learning the books of the Bible and understanding the meaning of the Ten Commandments) seem trivial in light of what they are facing today. As I reflect on the energy I poured into discussing Sunday school curriculum or debating worship styles, I shake my head.

Today, I can see I was part of the problem. I grieve my inability to predict today's challenges and am motivated to change the trajectory of forming faith for future generations.

Christian formation is a primary challenge the church faces today. Decades of research verify that our current approaches are not cultivating lifelong followers of Jesus,[3] or what Kenda Creasy Dean calls a "consequential faith."[4] Given the disruptions of the digital age and seismic shifts taking place in our religious landscape, this is not surprising. The approaches congregations have used and/or adapted were not designed for today's realities and are not reliable for the future. New approaches are needed.

Christian formation is a primary challenge the church faces today.

Faith formation is a complex issue, and these are complex times. Just like an earthquake exposed my assumptions and reoriented my world, forces are rocking foundational assumptions of faith formation and inviting the church to recalibrate. Recalibration requires transformational change that addresses identity and purpose. Walking leaders through a process for rethinking faith formation in today's complex times is the concern of this book. I have no illusion that the ideas presented here will provide congregations with a magic bullet, but my research suggests the time is ripe for local churches to take a leap of faith. The vibrancy of the church's future depends on its ability to form vital faith today. I have faith because people and communities surrounded and accompanied me in discovering a

Christian way of life. We are part of a larger story. God's people have faced obstacles before. Faith in the risen Christ is a bold proclamation that changes lives. It is time to courageously live into this proclamation.

I join this larger conversation as a curious learner, a contextual investigator, a church leader, and a mother. For thirty years, I have immersed myself in issues of faith formation—studying the terrain, listening to congregations, talking with people inside and outside the local church, and learning from and with colleagues. The world my children's faith is being formed in is nothing like the world in which my faith was formed. I wonder what God is up to and what we, as God's people, are called to be and do in this time. I am inquisitive and hopeful. Years from now, I imagine a future where God's people—my children and their children included—find meaningful communities of faith to wrestle with God's mysterious, majestic, and redemptive presence in the world and in their lives. Getting to that future from here is the task in front of us.

Faith is embodied, and faith formation is always contextual. There are no universal approaches, just shared practices. Because faith is formed in the world as well as within Christian communities, approaches to forming faith must be in conversation with contextual realities. Past faith formation models overlooked context, assuming Christianity was the dominant religion and environments changed slowly. Today's circumstances are different. While recent faith formation literature is attending to particular contextual shifts,[5] I have not found an overarching contextual approach to forming faith.

This book offers a contextual approach to forming faith within the particularities of the twenty-first century. It reminds the church of its call to form faith, offers an operating system that works with highly dynamic environments, and provides a process for custom-designing congregational faith formation ministries. Because faith formation is a common practice with a messy definition, this book also provides an understanding of faith formation. Faith formation is *the ways faith shapes people as they encounter God, others, and the world*. The aim of faith formation is *discovering a Christian way of life*, making the outside world as critical for forming faith as faith communities.

Mapping Dynamic Contexts

Maps are tools for navigating contexts. Their form and function have changed over the years. The early maps of the Babylonian world, dating back from 700 to 500 BCE, were inscribed on clay tablets and provided a picture of the entire world small enough to hold in your hand.[6] Maps in the late nineteenth century were scalable images based on latitude and longitude coordinates and on-the-ground exploring. GPS technology has expanded current mapping capabilities by integrating satellites, receivers, and computers. Now, mobile devices give us access to up-to-date maps around the world in the palm of our hands.

GPS is a tool designed for navigating highly dynamic environments. In a world where recalibrating is the norm, maps adapt and speak. This is good news and bad news. It's good news because GPS offers real-time navigation. Did it snow overnight? No need to worry, Siri can chart the fastest route to work. Encounter an accident on the way to a baseball game? Just punch in the coordinates and your favorite mapping app will reroute you. Need to find a drugstore? No problem, just turn on the shopping feature and Apple Maps will show you the nearest one. The bad news is people are losing their ability to read contexts. Farmers know how important it is to anticipate changing weather. Wilderness travelers know how to read the sky in order to distinguish a passing shower from a major storm. Relying solely on technology, travelers can easily miss contextual clues right in front of their eyes and find themselves surprised by disruptive forces. Navigating highly dynamic environments requires both GPS technology and the ability to read our environment.

Today's highly dynamic environment has been described with four powerful adjectives: volatile, uncertain, complex, and ambiguous—or VUCA. Whether or not you have heard of the concept of VUCA, you have likely experienced it. *Volatility* has to do with the accelerated rate of change. *Uncertainty* relates to the increase of surprises and inability to predict behavior and circumstances based on the past. *Complexity* names the decrease in cause-and-effect relationships, the multidimensional nature of challenges, and the increase in interdependency. *Ambiguity* points to the environment's mixed messages, making it difficult to read the present and forecast the future.

VUCA is the condition created as six mega-trends came together: globalization, technology, digitization, individualization, demographic change, and environmental crisis.[7] The acronym was first used in 1987 by the military to describe their experience at the end of the Cold War. By the early 2000s, the term was used within various disciplines to describe strategic leadership. Today, "VUCA is becoming the 'normal context' for leadership and requires leaders to adopt appropriate perspectives and skill sets."[8] This new normal is calling ministry leaders to recalibrate. Leading in a VUCA environment requires a different perspective, the ability to read contextual changes, and new practices.

Forming faith in a VUCA environment requires a GPS-like operating system that can recalibrate automatically and the capacity to read dynamic environments. Just like paper maps and atlases were designed for different conditions, many of our approaches to faith formation were designed for different eras. As the world becomes more fluid, as values shift and priorities change, and as new possibilities become available, approaches to forming faith must be agile and flexible. Navigating our VUCA environment is like journeying in the wilderness. In the wilderness, travelers work with basic tools, operate with different mindsets, and expect disruptions.

> Navigating our VUCA environment is like journeying in the wilderness.

Those of us navigating the first decades of the twenty-first century are living in uncharted territory. Traveling through this terrain requires a growing attentiveness, reorienting expectations, and acquiring new skills. It's inherently risky, and at times, it is uncomfortable. But we do not journey alone. God promises to be with us every step of the way, and traveling with others enhances our experience and expands our resources. Wilderness trails are less pronounced, making discerning the trail an expected part of the adventure. Setting direction, getting oriented, and learning to read ever-changing surroundings is how we find our way.

This is an exciting time, so lean into it and explore this uncharted territory. Let this book, with its activities and practices, be a guide for discovering an approach to faith formation that fits your context.

The Flow of the Book

"Journeying in the wilderness" is a metaphor for forming faith. Wilderness not only describes today's highly dynamic environment; it also sets the tone for the adventure of faith. An aspect of the metaphor is highlighted in each chapter along with a contemporary wilderness story and elements of faith formation. Each chapter also frames the journey of faith theologically and connects a biblical story to everyday life. Activities at the end of each chapter translate ideas into ministry contexts and draw on people's experiences. Practices anchor this work in our own formational encounters with God and others.

Chapter 1 *sets the stage* by introducing a contextual approach to faith formation and describing today's VUCA environment. This chapter suggests that navigating the uncertainty of today's environments is like navigating uncharted wilderness and invites everyone to adopt an explorer's mindset. The story of the Israelites wandering in the wilderness recognizes the formative power of wilderness experiences and God's presence in these times. Congregations are invited to rediscover their call to steward the future witness of the Christian faith.

Chapter 2 *orients the journey of faith* by naming what does not change—God's love and promised future. With faith as a living relationship with God and our call to love God and our neighbor, this chapter proposes that forming faith is accompanying people in discovering a Christian way of life. Two movements and four commitments allow God's people to orient their lives and find dynamic stability. The story of Jesus in the wilderness sheds light on how to claim our identity and navigate uncertainty. Congregations are challenged to reflect on their own understanding of faith formation.

Chapter 3 *places our call to love God and our neighbor in dialog* with forces disrupting today's context. Believing discernment happens on the way, this chapter recognizes that the church is unraveling from culture, unpacks five disruptive forces, and describes how to organize ourselves around our call. The story of the disciples being sent into the wilderness reminds us disruptions are part of faith. As peculiar people, Christians are free to live in solidarity with their neighbor and in the midst of paradox. Congregations are provided tools for reflecting on how disruptions are impacting their ministry context.

Chapter 4 *reimagines abundant living* by claiming God's love transforms us into co-creators with God. Working with a new operating system, this chapter demonstrates that learning from the future uncovers our blind spots, involves change, and includes playgrounds of possibility. The story of the good Samaritan points to the power of love in action. Congregations are encouraged to imagine abundant living and engage in experiments in their ministry setting.

Chapter 5 *proposes congregations become cruciform communities of hope* that join people in making meaning. As they accompany people in discovering a Christian way of life, congregations can introduce three types of practices: sanctuary, campfire, and outpost. The story of Paul's missionary journey recognizes that times in the wilderness are guided by the Spirit. Congregations conclude their contextualizing process by connecting previous activities into a customized approach to forming faith.

Activities personalize and translate the ideas of each chapter into specific contexts. Practices provide the scaffolding for being formed, informed, and transformed by God in the midst of this process by creating space for encountering God and our neighbor. These practices encourage participants to listen as the Spirit stirs, others speak, and we reflect.

Practices are used in this book in a particular way. Think about it like this: Both yoga and basketball involve practice, yet each views it differently. In basketball, practice prepares players. The game is the "real deal," and practice is preparatory. During practice, coaches run drills, do aerobic exercises, teach plays, and get teammates working together so teams are ready for the game. In yoga, practice is when a person engages in a series of yoga poses. A yogi, or instructor, creates the atmosphere, guides the practice, and gives suggestions (to the group and to individuals), but each person does their own practice. Yoga is not rehearsing for the real deal; it is the real deal. Yoga is a way of being that brings together the mind, body, and soul. Participants can read about, watch others do, and study yoga, but the only way to *do* yoga is to engage in the practice. Yoga is learned by doing. Beginners and experts alike practice alongside each other, continually learning as they go.

The practices in this book are like the practice of yoga. Ten practices are presented, two in each chapter, to accompany you in discovering a Christian way of life. Try them on, experiment with them, and feel free to engage them in any order. Mastery is not the goal; participation is.

A contextual approach to forming faith is an emergent process. Each chapter contributes to the process of finding a way forward. The book is presented in a linear fashion, but the flow is more iterative than straightforward. It is messy, and steps overlap. If you go forward and feel the need to circle back, by all means, do so. Moving through the process, hold each step as if you are juggling balls—loosely. Keep the big picture in mind, pay attention to each step, and be open to God's leading.

We are living in a time when the whole church, and every local church, is discerning its way forward. The commitment to slow down and reflect while learning new practices is key. This book is a resource. Enjoy the stories, embrace the metaphors, try the practices, and engage in the activities. It is a quick read, but read it slowly and with conversation partners so you can recalibrate in a way that fits your circumstance. I pray the Spirit of God moves among you both now and in the days ahead.

1

Welcome to the Wilderness: Embracing the Call

> All have faith in something; the question is, is it trust in the living God or in something else? Will our children be nurtured and transformed by the faith and community that trust and confess the God who calls us? Few questions are more urgent and significant for [the] church's life and mission.[1]

I recently came across our camping gear in the garage—Duluth packs, stuff sacks, tents, sleeping pads, and a camping stove. The smell brought back memories of canoe trips in the Boundary Waters Canoe Area (BWCA) in northern Minnesota. Memories of our girls, then in elementary school, learning the basics of camping and canoeing. Memories of meaningful campfires, bonding with friends, and surrounding our kids in community. Memories of time away, experiencing Sabbath while watching loons and majestic sunsets. Most of these memories are delightful, but wilderness adventures are also challenging. I remember battling powerful winds and torrential rain, getting lost and searching for campsites in the dark, and even a bear eating our food. That afternoon, the smells I associated with the wilderness allowed me to reflect on how formative those experiences were for our family.

Our camping gear reminded me of the difference between everyday life and being in the wilderness. In everyday life, it is easy to take things for granted. In the wilderness, it is important to know the basics and travel light. At home, turning on the faucet becomes routine, making it easy to forget about water's life-giving quality and beauty. In the wilderness, gathering and filtering water highlights the interdependency of our ecosystem and the vital role water plays. At home, resources are abundant and close at hand. In the wilderness, tools are limited, and good judgment saves lives. I know how to live in both environments, but each requires different competencies, has different rhythms, and draws on different mindsets. At the end of each wilderness adventure, I pack my wilderness mindset away with the camping gear—but what if forming faith in the twenty-first century is more like navigating the wilderness than being at home?

As a church leader, I am interested in how the church forms faith. Traveling the country, I find the current approaches to forming faith inadequate for today's complexities. People's questions today are different from previous generations; they are multilayered, complicated, and particular. Taking these up is not easy, especially if our primary vehicle is a forty-five-minute Sunday school session or a twelve-minute sermon, yet questions provide insights into people's experiences. The church's ability (or inability) to engage their questions and concerns is central to integrating faith into their lives. Adapting worship styles, changing programs, and creating innovative curriculum are not enough for addressing the challenges we face. We need another approach.

Society has changed, and the church is searching for a way forward. Trusted paths are not sufficient because life patterns and ministry conditions have been disrupted. What do these changes mean? What are congregations to do? Congregations make choices with the limited information they have. Hoping to do more good than harm, some focus on everyday demands, others hold on to maps from the past, and some bushwhack new trails. The decisions congregations make today impact the future; without guidance, these choices feel more like gambling than faithful leadership.

A Pivotal Moment

Faith is a living relationship with God shaped by our encounters with God, others, and the world. As an embodied faith, contextual concerns and driving forces explicitly or implicitly impact how faith is formed in each era. For the church to faithfully live its call to form faith in each generation, it must be attentive to the contextual realities of its day.

Think about the impact contextual realities had for Christians living in Germany during World War II. Christianity was the majority religion in Germany, with almost all of the country's sixty million people identifying with some expression of the Christian faith (forty million Protestant, twenty million Roman Catholic, and less than 1 percent Jewish).[2] Ecclesial, political, and social concerns were intertwined with Christianity, so thinking critically about faith challenged mainstream viewpoints, impacted social relationships, and had political ramifications. Imagine the potential conflict of loving your neighbor when your Jewish neighbor is labeled and discriminated against. Or think about the consequences of challenging the injustice of governmental actions when family and friends rely on and are privileged by its support.

Or what about the contextual realities of forming faith in the United States as it expanded west? As the Louisiana Purchase doubled the size of the country, attention shifted from transplanting European ideals into American soil to acquiring territory and creating a new nation. As an "experiment of liberty,"[3] the United States was greatly influenced by the religious beliefs woven into Manifest Destiny.[4] As the nation expanded, congregations were planted within newly established communities to share the gospel and serve the people. This partnership served the church well in many ways, but it also had a shadow side. The actions of white people, especially as they related to Native Americans and Mexicans, created mindsets and obstacles regarding land, unity, and difference, which still remain today.

Contextual dimensions impact the formation of faith in the present and in the future. Forming faith is always contextual, and the multilayered nature of contextualization is one reason forming faith is a dynamic enterprise.

This is a pivotal contextual moment. Highly dynamic, today's context is a result of several disruptive forces coming together. Simultaneously independent and interdependent, these forces have created what Thomas Friedman calls an "age of acceleration."[5] The rate and scope of these forces are making today's environment volatile, uncertain, complex, and ambiguous (VUCA).[6] Independently, any one of these interrupts, but collectively, they are altering our way of life. Unless we work with our context, our modus operandi will be survival instead of living abundantly.

> Highly dynamic, today's context is a result of several disruptive forces coming together.

Understanding the multilayered nature of today's context is not a simple task. Yet there is no going back; this is the context in which the church is called to form faith. As these disruptive forces stress current approaches beyond their capacity, the church can use this as an opportunity to recalibrate.

Congregations can lead the church into the future. Congregations that are clear about their call, work with contextual realities, and open themselves to new ways of thinking can find a new stability to guide them into the future. As people of faith hold fast to God's love and join God's activity in the world, they discover a Christian way of living in any environment, even a highly dynamic one. God is steadfast, and communities of faith have adapted to cultural shifts before. The future will not look like the past, but ministry leaders can develop new capacities. Congregations are positioned to be on the front line, welcoming the emerging future. This is an opportune moment. Are you open to discerning another way? If so, set your eyes toward the future, open yourself to God, and gather with a community to discern the trail together.

God brings order out of chaos and life out of death. God's deepest desire is for us, and all of creation, to live abundantly. Second Corinthians 5:17 states that life in Christ makes us new creations. Isaiah 43:19 reminds us God always finds a way, even in uncertain, wilderness times. This is good news. God continues to be active, making the world new. Can you see it? Our way forward begins by relying on God.

Discerning the way forward depends on God because God is the one who forms, transforms, and informs faith. The church joins God by participating in God's incredible mission of loving the world. Placing God front and center frees the church to hold its commitments, assumptions, and models loosely. Working with and within contextual realities to form faith, God's people adopt a learning posture, return to the basics, and become curious about others and the world. We go into the future with a spirit of adventure, embracing mystery, facing unexpected challenges, and uncertain of where it will take us. On the way, we reimagine abundant life and discover, again or for the first time, what it means to form faith in concert with our context.

Investing in the Future

Faith formation pays attention to present realities, but it also takes into account the past and the future. Present challenges in dialog with Christian traditions and God's promised future remind us we are part of a bigger story. For centuries, people have shared stories that witness to the God of Abraham, Isaac, and Jacob. This God is the one who creates, redeems, and sustains life and is the one with whom we live eternally. The local church incarnates this interplay of time as "an historic, tradition-bearing community of faith"[7] where "faith is expressed, transformed, and made meaningful"[8] and life is directed to a promised future.

Witnessing to faith and cultivating faith-filled lives are central to following God. You and I know God's love because of faithful witnesses in the past. Faithful people have taught, engaged in, and recalibrated faith practices to keep them alive over centuries. The Old Testament tells how the Hebrews, a small but mighty people, understood themselves as God's chosen people, called to bless others. New Testament Christians were deliberate in sharing the gospel and expanding the church. They knew their future was not guaranteed and felt an urgency to spread God's love from Jerusalem to the ends of the earth. As they birthed and nurtured communities of faith, the church grew, and God's love spread.

Witnessing to faith and cultivating faith-filled lives are central to following God.

Perhaps it is time for congregations to rediscover their call to steward the future witness to the Christian faith. As in other eras, there is an urgency to this call. Christianity's future is not tied to the viability of the institutional church but does rely on people of faith being in relationship with God and joining God's mission. Because the church is always just one generation away from being extinct, it cannot take its future for granted. It is time to awaken local churches and enliven communities of faith to participate with God in forming meaningful, life-transforming faith. Doing so invests in the future.

The majority of approaches to forming faith today were developed for an environment where Christianity was the majority religion. This environment assumed society operated with a Christian ethos and believed congregations supported society by nurturing, supporting, and teaching the Christian faith. Christianity's partnership with society was mutually beneficial. Christianity influenced societal ethics while society cultivated norms that reinforced particular Christian values and commitments. Business schedules, for example, provided a pattern for life that encouraged Christian faith practices. Stores opened late on Sundays and were closed on Christian holidays, allowing Christians to worship and participate in special religious activities. While the United States was founded on the separation of church and state, for most of its history, it has operated with a de facto church-and-state partnership. Cultivating a Christian way of life within an environment where Christianity is normative makes forming faith a majority practice.

The assumptions underlying a church-and-state partnership can lull the church into a distorted view of itself. Within such an environment, congregations can lose their capacity to witness to God's story and share God's overflowing love with others. Church leaders can stop teaching the basics of faith because they assume everyone knows about Christianity and the Bible. And followers of Jesus can become overly focused on congregational life rather than on God's presence in the world and in their lives. Forming faith within a majority view can turn faith into a passive activity, with little urgency or meaning. As Christianity competes with other religions and with societal factors in the United States, the Christian church must reimagine forming faith from a minority perspective.

Today's world is a complex constellation of cultures. The diversity and richness within this constellation are a gift, yet navigating the complexity is difficult. Learning to be Christian in a context that does not speak the language of the Christian faith, does not have overlapping values, and/or does not reinforce Christian practices requires new approaches. Where do we begin?

Finding My Way

At fifty-two, I decided to pursue an adventure. The weekend before my birthday, I explored my neighborhood on my bike. As I made my way from my suburban home to the country, I remembered my love for cycling. With the sun on my face and wind in my hair, I forgot about time and the stress of work, and my spirit was renewed. While biking, I reflected on the hundreds of trails in Minnesota, and by the time I returned home, I had committed to biking fifty-two different routes before I put my bike away for the season.

The next day, I spread out my Minneapolis/St. Paul bike map on my kitchen table and started scoping out rides. Over the next seven days, I biked a few trails and made a list of others I wanted to try. Quickly overwhelmed with possibilities, I had to get more strategic. So, I found some biking apps, replaced my paper maps with the bike feature of Google Maps, and developed a pattern. For each ride, I drove to the trailhead, unpacked my bike, explored some unknown route, and returned to the car. Then I snapped a photo and posted it on Instagram with #BikeMN52. Things were falling into place. There was just one more thing—I needed a different attitude.

I have been biking since childhood. Biking provided me freedom and kept me active. When I turned fifteen, I saved for a 10-speed Schwinn road bike. That bike got me to my friends' houses and introduced me to the sport of cycling; my Schwinn took me across Minnesota on my first three-day bike ride and helped me successfully finish many triathlons. Now, thirty years later, I have upgraded my bike several times and participated in many bike treks and races. Biking has become a sport for me, with goals around speed and distance. But weeks into this adventure, those goals were not working. Exploring new bike trails was not efficient. Getting to trails took time. Riding unknown territory required frequent stops and checking my map or asking for directions. Evaluating each ride by my average miles per hour or distance took the joy out of the adventure. My past understanding was not working—I needed a new mindset.

As pictures of my rides populated my social media feed, people started asking me about my adventure. My responses revealed two things. First, I loved exploring bike trails in Minnesota. The beauty of each ride captured my attention, introducing me to new places and giving me a fresh perspective on familiar places. Second, I loved talking to people about biking. Posting my rides made my adventure public, and people were interested. Avid bikers and novices alike commented on my posts and/or asked questions. In responding to their posts, I learned I had a passion for helping others discover the joy of biking, so I started sharing information about my rides and inviting others to join me. By mid-July, I had a new mindset—I had become an explorer. For the rest of the summer, exploring Minnesota bike trails became my thing. Each ride was a chance to discover a new trail, develop new capacities, and embrace curiosity. #BikeMN52 was an impulsive decision that changed my worldview.

A Discovery Process

What is an explorer mindset? According to psychologist Carol Dweck, all humans are born with curiosity and the capacity for learning known as a growth mindset. Children operate from this growth mindset, but many adults lose this capacity as their mindset becomes fixed. Mindsets filter our view of the world, and how we see the world impacts all areas of life. An explorer mindset sees the world through a growth mindset—curious and open to learning. In dynamic environments, a growth mindset is imperative.

Our natural abilities do not dictate our true potential; what matters is how we develop them. Learning, effort, interests, and environments all influence what we become. People with growth mindsets understand that. For them, failure provides clues for development because it points to specific places of learning and being stretched. Internal motivation and a supportive environment help people reach their full potential.[9] People with fixed mindsets see failure as a setback because they focus on achieving an outcome and believe intelligence and personality are set. Assessments shape the self-understanding of people with fixed mindsets, leaving much of adulthood focused on proving or protecting themselves.[10]

Tests and people influence our formation and can shift people's mindsets from growth to fixed. The results of an IQ test, for example, can become a defining characteristic for some people. One test, designed to measure particular competencies (in this case, "a person's problem-solving and reasoning abilities"[11]), is not designed to limit one's potential over a lifetime. Tests and assessments are just tools that, when used well, help us understand our God-given abilities or natural bents.

People—parents, coaches, teachers, music instructors, mentors, and/or counselors—can also shift people's mindset. As mirrors, people give each other clues about what they see and hear. As others' words are internalized, they form our self-understanding. Praising talent, intellect, and/or prizes rewards fixed mindset thinking, while praising learning, effort, and/or energy reinforces growth mindset thinking. The messages we send others about failure or mistakes can focus on performance or learning. We all have the ability to filter the messages others send, yet over time, words influence the environments that shape our mindset.

What has shaped your mindset? Were you praised or criticized for your intellectual, musical, athletic, and/or relational capacities? Have you learned something new or discovered a capacity you did not have as a child? We all have limitations, but do you believe you can continue to learn and grow? Limiting our capacity to learn and narrowing how we see our God-given abilities close us off to God's ongoing work in us. God created us with a growth mindset.

A life of faith is a lifelong journey of becoming. We are made new in Christ. Redeemed through Christ's death and resurrection, we are continually transformed by God's grace. Every day God wants us to know we are loved beyond measure. Becoming the person God created us to be does not stop at a particular age or developmental stage; it is a lifelong journey. Being Christian entails discovering what it is to be God's children, heirs to God's kingdom, and participants in God's mission. Belonging to God anchors us and gives us our identity. God's unfolding kingdom is a taste of God's future. God's mission of loving the world gives life purpose and makes us co-creators of the future. A life of faith is a lifelong

Becoming the person God created us to be . . . is a lifelong journey.

journey of discovery. How do we embrace the becoming nature of faith?

The world pushes us toward a fixed mindset. In fact, we are so conditioned to define ourselves by outcomes and goals that we might not even see it. Educational systems can emphasize outcomes over becoming, and so can Christian education. Christian education is one approach to forming faith. It has provided thoughtful models for learning the Bible and intentional thinking about the development of faith, but it has also separated learning about faith from the rest of ministry and everyday life. As Christian education became formalized, people began equating learning *about* faith, in time-bound activities at church, with *forming* faith. This mindset shifted the primary location of nurturing faith from the home to congregations and made developmentally appropriate programs the primary means of faith formation. Not only did learning about faith become packaged in "officially approved" programs, but faith became separated from life outside of church. This approach gave the impression that forming faith requires formal curriculums, learning goals, and/or confirmation requirements. This approach to forming faith is driven by the church's agenda and focuses primarily on studying doctrine and the Bible. Within this mindset, curiosity and complex questions create awkward situations and push teachers out of their comfort zone. If our faith formation systems focus primarily on outcomes related to formal curriculums and learning goals, we create fixed mindset environments.

Imagine faith in a growth mindset environment. Rather than emphasizing correct answers and certain behaviors, questioning would be encouraged, learning moments embraced, and the becoming nature of faith highlighted. The curriculum would emerge as much from daily life and relationships as from studying doctrine. A growth mindset approach connects faith with everyday life, sees formation as experiential, and understands catechisms and biblical texts as lifelong conversation partners. Within this mindset, forming faith is an open process of discovery, not information to acquire or outcomes to attain. Can the church reorient its faith formation mindset toward this type of discovery process?

Being Christian is less about articulating a set of ideas and more about loving God and our neighbor. The first reinforces compartmentalization; the second integrates into everyday life. Being Christian is a journey of love. We love others because God loved us first. Love is anything but predictable. As we love others, welcome strangers, forgive friends, and serve those in need, we embody God's love in the world. This becoming journey is a relational one centered on God's love. God's promised future sets the direction, practices anchor and sustain us, and the world is the primary location where it is expressed. The dynamic interplay of God, others, and the world forms us and our faith.

As our lives unfold, people, experiences, and God form us. We are not the same today as we were yesterday, and tomorrow we will be different from today because God created us as becoming beings. Our past, personalities, talents, and gifts contribute to who we are, but God's love grounds our identity and gives us our worth. God created within us the ability to learn, change, and start anew. We are becoming people.

A Radical Claim

Each Sunday, Christians make a radical claim—God is alive. The God of Abraham, Isaac, Jacob, and Moses is present with us today. Gathered in worship, people of faith pray, trusting in God's healing power. Pastors point to God's activity as they proclaim the good news of the gospel. God's Spirit unites the hearts and lives of families, friends, and strangers as congregations praise God in song and fellowship. God shows up as crosses are made on foreheads at the baptismal font, people eat bread and drink wine around God's table, and neighbors open their heart and care for the needs of others. Through these ordinary practices, communities of faith claim God's presence as they point to God's continued activity in our lives and in the world.

Gathered in community, people of faith expect God to be present, but how about when we are scattered? When was the last time you expected God to be present as you washed dishes, mowed the grass, dropped kids off at school, bought groceries, or did laundry? While it is natural to recognize God's presence when we gather, it is harder to imagine God's presence in our daily activities. Being attentive to God's presence can be turned off like a light switch the minute we leave the church building. In the world, our minds are easily preoccupied with daily demands, and God can be distanced from our relationships, concerns, and activities. Still, Christians claim God is present in the world. Maybe it's time to notice God's activity all around us.

In my young adult years, I thought faith required me to come to God. This understanding overemphasized my side of the relationship. Within this mindset, I worked hard to set aside time to talk to God and serve my neighbor. Much of that time was rich, but the focus was on me and my behavior instead of God's presence. Over time, my patterns changed. Married with kids and working full-time, I got busy and spent less time alone with God. Because my focus was on me, I felt guilty. Integrating faith into life outside of church activities was hard, and I felt like a failure most days.

Recently, I discovered a different mindset. Rather than reduce a life of faith to a constellation of activities, my focus shifted to God's activity. Because God is present everywhere, I can look for God anywhere and at all times. Now my actions flowed from God's, not the other way around. What if discovering a Christian way of life focused primarily on what God is doing? As a journey of becoming, a life of faith is as much about being curious and anticipating God's presence as it is about the time spent in Bible study or on a mission trip. As scouts of God's ongoing activity in the world, Christians spot God's activity and tell others. We confess in our creeds a belief in a God who creates, redeems, and sustains life. These activities are ongoing and all around us. Confessing these beliefs is one thing; noticing and joining them is another.

Now my actions flowed from God's, not the other way around.

A life of faith is an adventure that calls for an explorer's mindset. Navigating today's highly dynamic context moves this adventure from predictable pathways and the security of established systems to untamed territory without clear signs and routes. Embracing this becoming journey means stepping into unpredictable terrain and adopting an explorer mindset. God's people have been here before. What can we learn from their stories and experiences?

Journeying in the Wilderness

God promised the Israelites a new land after being captives in Egypt for four hundred years. To get there, they had to journey through the wilderness. After centuries of living in a foreign country, the promises made to Abraham, Isaac, and Jacob had become a faint dream. Before the Israelites would have the opportunity to live their own way of life, they had to navigate the wilderness. What does their story teach us?

First, *our ability to notice God is not the same as God's presence.* God did not speak to the Israelites while they lived in Egypt, but God did bless them. In fact, God's blessing, specifically by increasing the population, was what made Pharaoh, the ruler of Egypt, fearful of them. God's love for the Israelites was consistent. God saw their circumstances and had compassion for them. They just had difficulty seeing it.

I can imagine why the Israelites found it hard to believe God was present, because God acted in surprising ways. God called Moses, a man with a complicated history, to lead them. He was not the person the Israelites would have chosen to be their leader. Moses was born to a Levite woman, raised by an Egyptian princess, and married to the daughter of a Midianite priest.

And the way God called Moses was strange, too. In the middle of Moses's ordinary day, God spoke to him through a burning bush. As Moses followed God's mission, God acted through frogs, lice, locusts, hail, and by Moses raising his staff. These were strange ways for God to communicate. When the Israelites were in the wilderness, God guided them with a cloud by day and fire by night. God provided manna to feed them and commandments to form them, but again, that is not what the people expected. God's presence was continuous, but it was not predictable. Humans, with our limitations and short-sightedness, struggle to see God, but that does not mean God is not present.

Have you ever wondered about God's presence in your life? Have you doubted God's promise to provide for your needs? Has God communicated to you in an unusual way? Maybe God has not been revealed to you in burning bushes, manna from heaven, or stone tablets, but God is present. And just like God provided for the Israelites, God will provide for you. Our ability to see and hear God is different from God's presence and provision.

Second, *faithful followers recognize God's heart*. Throughout the Israelites' time in captivity, stories were told of God interacting with Abraham, Isaac, and Jacob. When God spoke to Moses, Moses recognized God's nature from the stories he had heard. Moses knew it was God not because he had heard God's voice before, but because he knew God's heart.

The forty years the Israelites wandered in the wilderness were years of formation. While Moses knew God's heart, many of the Israelites did not. Before the Israelites entered the promised land, they had to hear the stories and revive their relationship with God. That work took a whole generation. Many of the Israelites did not make it to the promised land, but they did play a key role in forming the next generation.

How are you at recognizing God? Do you know God with your head and heart? What does it mean to be part of a community whose ancestors can be traced back centuries? How is God inviting your community of faith to form faith for the future? In the wilderness, knowing God's heart is important for discerning our way forward. Sharing stories of faith and God's faithfulness across time is one way to discover God's character.

Third, *God calls and sends; leaders act in faith.* God saw a new future for the Israelites. Their wilderness journey required letting go of everything they knew and trusting God to lead them. God called Moses, but Moses was hesitant. Who could blame him? Moses offered excuses, named his fears, and doubted his abilities, yet God still called Moses. And that call was enough. In time, Moses embraced his mission and acted in faith. Moses did not need to know the future; he only had to trust God would point the way. As we travel in wilderness territory, God sends, and we trust, and that is enough. Over time, all the Israelites came to know and trust God, but in the beginning, a leader needed to step forward.

When we feel like captives, freedom comes when we let go and open ourselves to another way. Moses was willing to drop what he knew and open himself to follow God. The Israelites were released from Pharaoh's rule, but freedom only came as they embraced God's way of life and learned to love others as God loved them.

How has God called you to step out in faith? Can you relate to Moses's reluctance? Does knowing that God calls you to lead give you comfort? What would embracing God's way of life look like in your setting? What would happen if your leadership focused more on God and less on your abilities? Stepping out in faith requires letting go of past notions and opening ourselves to move forward trusting God. Leaders act on faith.

Wilderness periods shape us in significant ways and prepare us for what lies ahead. The Israelites could not have governed themselves in a new land without this time in the wilderness. It must have been scary to leave Egypt and step out in faith. There were many hardships and new learnings along the way, but God used their time in the wilderness for a purpose greater than they could imagine.

How has God called you to step out in faith?

Embracing the Call—It Is Time

My kids are now young adults. Looking at their lives, I understand how truly formative those BWCA canoe trips were. As faithful, independent women, they are discerning how to make a difference in the world. As they love God and their neighbors, they are discovering their identity as children of God and a vision for living abundantly. I see their unique gifts shaping their becoming journey. Their faith has been formed by participating in and adapting practices from our family and various communities of faith. As their mom, I marvel at their wisdom and wonder about their future. Yet I also question our choices in light of their future. The world is changing so fast. Have we done enough to prepare them for the uncertainties that lie ahead? Are we asking the right questions in these pivotal years? Are our relationships the right mix of safety and challenge? Do they know God truly loves them?

Each generation is called to witness to the risen Christ and accompany people in discovering a Christian way of life. This is not just the call of parents; it is the call of all of us. While this calling does not change, the approaches we use will. Faith is lived in particular times and places, requiring that we continually discover how to engage contextual realities. We are becoming people. May we step out in faith and discern a pathway for forming faith in the midst of twenty-first-century contextual realities.

Practice of Listening

"Listening is not the same as hearing."[12] Hearing is a physical ability; listening is "a conscious process."[13] Listening takes in stories, ideas, feelings, and frustrations using verbal, nonverbal, and contextual clues. Humans are wired to listen and also have a need to be heard. We teach children to listen, yet most adults stop developing this practice. Studies show most adults underutilize their listening capacity (on average, people only listen at about 25 percent efficiency[14]) and feel no need to improve.

Listening requires focus, emotional attention, physical engagement, and reading the environment. The capacity to listen well builds understanding, connections, and self-worth, as well as cultivating clear communication, enhancing trust, and aiding in conflict resolution. Listening involves a range of experiences and is a practice woven into all areas of our daily life. Unfortunately, it seems to be disappearing in our digitally mediated, 24/7 world. Our context is noisy, and we live connected to our devices, making it extremely difficult to listen with our full, undivided attention. As a practice exercised less and less in society, what if listening was reframed as a spiritual practice?

Listening as spiritual practice shifts our focus from ourselves to others. Listening to others honors them as a unique one-of-a-kind person created by God. Focusing on others creates the opportunity to go deeper into another's experience and understand what lies below the surface. Listening with an empathetic ear provides insight into others' feelings; we recognize another's humanity and have the opportunity to care for another. Listening with an interpretive ear seeks to reflect on life, clarifying experiences, accompanying others in meaning-making. Listening with a theological ear seeks to discern God's movement in another's life and allows God to work in and through us. In other words, listening connects people and cultivates relationships and has a transforming capacity, not only within individuals, but also within communities.[15]

> Listening as spiritual practice shifts our focus from ourselves to others.

What does transformational listening entail? Listening with a transformative ear allows current norms and prevailing assumptions to be challenged by opening space for another's point of view. This type of listening requires the listener to bracket their own understanding in order to fully hear another. Through dialog and questioning, the listener entertains another's perspective as valid, even if it differs from their own. When done well, both the listener and the speaker are changed. This practice is important in communities with a high degree of difference that is committed to honoring diverse perspectives. What drives both individuals and communities to participate is something bigger than themselves—a shared mission and/or vision. While transformative listening is relational, it is more than pastoral care and effective communication; it changes people and communities.

Transformational listening has a ripple effect. As space is opened and relationships are deepened, new ways of thinking become possible. Learning from this type of listening has the potential to be transferred from one area of life to another.[16] For example, developing transformational listening within a community with diverse theological understandings may allow participants to listen differently to family members or co-workers with diverse points of view. As congregations create the conditions for this type of listening, they foster environments where people feel safe and which expand people's ability to be present with others in ways that stand out in society.

How might congregations do this? It takes intentional practice. You might begin by drawing people into the present moment. This may involve a minute of silence or having people take a few deep breaths. Invite people to put aside whatever is preoccupying their mind and open themselves to those in the room. As you listen to another, become curious. Pay attention to verbal and nonverbal clues; focus on what the other person is trying to communicate. Are you able to imagine their perspective? How can you deepen your understanding? How can you reflect back to them what you are hearing and invite their own reflection? What conditions are important for you to focus on the speaker? What other practices can be incorporated to enhance your exchange? Would prayer be appropriate? Would having another person join the conversation be helpful? Would guidelines help create boundaries?

Listening to another's story is a sacred practice. Developing our capacity to listen, especially across diverse perspectives and in the midst of conflict, is a way faith can be integrated into everyday life. As congregations cultivate listening—empathetically, interpretively, and transformationally—they connect the times God's people gather with being scattered in the world, creating space for the Holy Spirit to enter into the most fundamental parts of our lives—our relationships.

Practice of Reflecting on Experience

Imagine this: The day starts with your mother calling with an update on her health. Your workday is filled with meetings. Your daughter texts you at lunch asking to talk after dinner. After work, you remember you need groceries. The gas tank is empty, so you stop at the gas station only to get an incorrect amount of change from the cashier, and then it happens—you lose it. Having navigated challenges all day, you release your pent-up energy on this poor stranger. At home, you draw on reserves to make dinner, and almost forget to talk with your daughter.

This day, with its mix of ordinary and extraordinary experiences, could represent what happens in the harried life of many people. Filled with cognitive, emotional, and relational demands, we rely on our personal frameworks, mental habits, patience, and stamina to get by. What happens when life provides no opportunity to pause and reflect?

Jack Mezirow and colleagues write that "a defining condition of being human is that we have to understand the meaning of our experiences."[17] To understand our relationships and daily encounters, we must develop the ability to reflect and set aside time to do it. In this age of acceleration, dedicating ourselves to reflecting on experience goes against the flow, yet without it, our ability to make meaning and live abundantly is hampered.

As becoming people, Christians lean into God's promised future. Reflection allows us to put the present in conversation with the past and future. As God's love and promised future become part of our reflection, making meaning becomes holy, life-changing work. Reflecting on experience gets us in touch with our mental state and helps us consider our emotions while also looking at our agency and impact on others. Reflecting on experience guides us in processing situations in order to understand what is happening *around us* and *within us*. Our human tendency is to focus solely on our wants and needs, but reflection makes it possible for us to step outside ourselves to see situations through other perspectives.

Institutions used to help us do this work. They offered frameworks and communities that engaged us in reflective practices and helped us develop these capacities. As our attachment to institutions loosens, many of us are left without frameworks, practices, guides, and/or communities. Ironically, this loosening is happening in a time when human beings need to be "more conscious of [themselves], more social, more culturally wise, and more innovative in taking action."[18]

Developing our ability to reflect critically on experiences is uniquely human. Vital to this human development is making visible our operating framework or "structure of assumptions and expectations through which we filter sense impressions."[19] Operating frameworks exist so we can read situations and exchanges quickly. But are our operating frameworks fitting for this time? Are they guiding us toward abundant living? Shedding light on our operating framework allows us to see what "selectively shapes and delimits perception, cognition, feelings, and disposition by predisposing our intentions, expectations, and purposes."[20] In other words, seeing our operating framework reveals the filters we use to understand the world around us. Are those filters aligned with God's promised future?

Developmental theorists recognize that humans have the capacity to grow across their lifespan. Unlike child and youth development, adult development is related to learning and active reflection, not simple biology. Robert Kegan and Lisa Laskow Lahey, scholars in adult development, understand it as the "gradual evolution of people's meaning-making systems and psychological capacities."[21] Kegan and Laskow Lahey's research shows adults can increase their mental capacity, though most do not. Of their three stages of adult development, most (over 50 percent) are in the first level, called *socialized mind.* At this level, people are shaped by their personal environment, and they express themselves primarily through relationships. About one-third fall into the second level, called *self-authoring mind.* Here, some have developed belief systems and the ability to make choices apart from their environment. Only a few (less than 1 percent) are in the third level, called *self-transforming mind.* Persons in this level have a developed ideology (or belief system), are open to new ideas, are interdependent, and can handle contradictions.[22] Developing through the stages increases one's ability to process complexity. Today complexity exists in all areas of our life, and our VUCA environment demands "innovation, self-management, personal responsibility, and self-direction"[23] from all of us.

Reflecting on action takes many forms. Each type brings to light habits, frameworks, commitments, and concerns. Integrating reflective practices into our daily routine deepens and strengthens us, as it also reorients us "to the needs of others, the needs of those who are suffering, and ways we can use our knowledge and position to impact positive change."[24] In *Visionary Leadership in a Turbulent World*, Jennifer Moss Breen names six types of reflection: *anticipatory*, *in-the-moment*, *technical*, *personalistic*, *deliberative*, and *critical.*[25]

Integrating reflective practices into our daily routine deepens and strengthen us

Let me highlight one: *critical reflection.* We all have blind spots, and critical reflection provides a process for exposing these so we can grow and take action. Edgar Schein offers a simple model for critically reflecting on action—the ORJI model. It has four components: "We observe (O), we react emotionally to what we have observed (R), we analyze, process, and make judgments based on our observations and feelings (J), and we behave overtly in order to make something happen—we intervene (I)."[26] Each component brings in new data that provides understanding and the opportunity to change. Because "we block out a great deal of information that is potentially available if it does not fit our needs, expectations, preconceptions, and prejudgments,"[27] stepping back and reflecting on this loop gives us a bigger picture.

An example illustrates the ORJI process: A young couple with two young children moves in next door. You notice an awkwardness in your encounters with the husband. His wife travels frequently for work, so he stays home with their children. You encounter him and the children often—at the park, school functions, and the YMCA. Upon reflection, you observe that this dad is often the only "at-home" dad at these places (O) and remember the uncomfortable feeling you have each time you talk (R). Unsure about that feeling, you process what is happening and conclude he is the only stay-at-home dad you know, and you do not know what to talk about (J). This realization reveals the gender bias you have around at-home parents. With this new understanding, you decide to get to know the dad better and set up a play date (I). During that time, you learn more about him, and future conversations become less awkward.

There are many constructive ways to reflect on experience. Some are simple, while others are more time consuming. The goal of reflecting on experience is making meaning so we can live abundantly as children of God.

> What reflective practices are you already doing? How might reflecting on action become part of your becoming who God created you to be? What practices contribute to your ongoing development and that of your community of faith? Who might join you in exercising this practice?

Activities

1. *Engaging Scripture*—Read through the book of Exodus. In particular, pay attention to the three themes highlighted in this chapter. You can read through the entire book or parts by theme.

   Theme #1—God's presence—areas to be attentive to: Exodus 1; 2:23–25; 3; 13:17–18; 14:30–31; 17:1–7; and 40:34–38.

   Theme #2—God's heart—Chapters 3 and 33–34.

   Theme #3—God calls and sends—Exodus 3; 6:28–7:7; 28:1–5; and 29:42–46.

   Share your thoughts with the group. What stood out? What surprised you? What did you not know about this story? Using the questions in this chapter, discuss each of the three themes.

2. *Naming and Claiming God's Presence*—Our ability to notice God is separate from God being present. Just

like God was with the Israelites as they wandered in the wilderness, God is with us every day. There may not be a cloud guiding us by day or fire by night, but there are signs of God's presence in the world. Practice being scouts for God's presence by looking for God's activity around you. The church I attend has a practice of people sharing "God moments." Each time a ministry team gathers—for example, after handing out food at the food shelf—they begin by sharing how they saw God at work. The sharing may describe a time serving, an experience with their family, or a situation when out grocery shopping. Sharing "God moments" reminds people God is active among us, names the ways God is active, and provokes people of faith to look for God in their everyday life.

3. *Audit Your Current Approach to Faith Formation*—Name the current work your ministry is doing around faith formation or tending to the ways faith shapes our encounters with God, others, and the world to get a picture of your congregational approach. This can be done in a meeting (putting all the ideas on paper) or in between meetings (using a shared document like Google Docs). The matrix below might serve as a template to get the group started. After you have collected all the data, reflect on what you see.

	Ages Involved	**Contribution to Faith Formation**	**Notes**
Fellowship	Babies Preschool Elementary Teens Young Adults Adults Senior Adults		
Learning	Babies Preschool Elementary Teens Young Adults Adults Senior Adults		
Leadership	Babies Preschool Elementary Teens Young Adults Adults Senior Adults		

	Ages Involved	**Contribution to Faith Formation**	**Notes**
Service	Babies Preschool Elementary Teens Young Adults Adults Senior Adults		
Community Engagement	Babies Preschool Elementary Teens Young Adults Adults Senior Adults		
Faith in Daily Life	Babies Preschool Elementary Teens Young Adults Adults Senior Adults		

2

Finding Dynamic Stability: GPS for the Journey

> Within a context of volatility and uncertainty, it is incredibly helpful to have a clear road of the right direction, even if the path ahead is not altogether clear.[1]

My first year in youth ministry, I led a group of seventh-grade boys on a BWCA canoe trip. The group consisted of four boys, myself, and a college-aged guide; I was the oldest at twenty-four. None of the boys had been on a canoe trip before, and I was excited to introduce them to the BWCA.

Our adventure began at Wilderness Canoe Base, a Lutheran camp at the end of the Gunflint Trail on Seagull Lake. The evening we arrived, we prepared our supplies, had a short training session, and reviewed our route. The next morning, as the sun brightened, it did not take long before our canoes were in the water. The energy was high, and we were on our way.

Seagull Lake is a large lake, about five miles from one end to the other. With many islands and a rugged shoreline, it's a bit tricky to navigate. As we left camp and paddled into the main body of the lake, it hit us—the wind. Tucked behind a small island, our camp was sheltered from this tremendous force. Out on the lake, we were fully exposed. With a group of novice canoers, this could be a rocky start to our adventure. Heads down, each of us began paddling as hard as we could. There was no time for coaching; every canoe would have to figure out how to make their way to the other end of the lake. Our canoe tried zigging and zagging. Another crossed the main body to hug the shoreline. The other had no strategy at all. Somehow, we all made it across the lake to the bay of our first portage.

Facing the shoreline, the portage should have been directly in front of us. I, however, could not see it. The canoe guide did not see it. The boys could not see it. Floating in the bay, we were relieved to have survived the wind without swamping a canoe, but now we had to find the portage. We got out the map and compared it to what we saw on the shoreline. Something was not right.

Navigating the Wilderness

Our journey of faith can feel like my experience on Seagull Lake. We set out excited, only to discover we're not prepared. As our enthusiasm fades, we press on. Facing obstacles one by one, our confidence grows, only to dissipate when we find ourselves disoriented and in unfamiliar terrain. My experience on Seagull Lake made it clear our group had much to learn about navigating the wilderness.

Within our contemporary world, we have been socialized to be suspicious of the unknown and to domesticate unruly environments. Privileging safety and security, we are conditioned to control our surroundings and avoid risk. When unexpected conditions arise, this approach to life is tested and its limitations exposed. Should we open ourselves to other options or retreat to our previous ways?

Life is messy and unpredictable, filled with unknowns and unexpected twists and turns. Experience tells us life decisions cannot be reduced to probability statistics, and relationships cannot be evaluated by risk-management formulas. Yet, our desire for certainty makes us cautious and wary of new approaches. Living full, abundant lives is complex in any environment, to say nothing about a highly dynamic one. Navigating ever-changing terrain requires not only a new mindset but also particular tools and capacities.

Living full, abundant lives is complex in any environment.

In the wilderness, travelers need a reliable navigational system to go with their explorer mindset. The capacities and tools created for steady environments are less trustworthy in environments where circumstances are continually shifting. Traveling in the wilderness requires approaches that can recalibrate as the environment changes or a navigational system designed for dynamic stability. Two capacities provide the core for such a system. The first is *setting direction.* A clear direction allows travelers to set a course, create a plan, and make adjustments along the way. While setting direction has always been important, in today's VUCA environment, it is imperative. In stable environments, travelers can rely on signs and markers strategically placed throughout the terrain to guide them. In wilderness terrain, travelers are responsible for reading the landscape and staying aligned with their desired direction. More of an art than a science, setting direction is a key capacity in dynamic environments because without it we don't know where we want to go.

The second core capacity is *getting oriented.* Getting oriented is the ability to read the current location and put it into dialog with the direction we want to go. In familiar territory, we rely on routines, common pathways, and steady landmarks to get oriented. In unfamiliar territory, the responsibility for identifying reference points and reading environmental clues lands on travelers. Compasses are simple tools wilderness travelers use to get oriented, because they work with environmental forces. As compasses find north, travelers get their bearings and can locate themselves. As our twenty-first-century environment becomes more unpredictable and less familiar, identifying reference points and learning to read environmental clues become increasingly critical. What does this mean for forming faith?

Faith's Navigational System

A life of faith is like journeying in the wilderness. Given faith's unpredictable nature and our highly dynamic environment, people of faith need a navigational system created for dynamic stability. Just as a compass orients travelers, people of faith need a reliable reference point and direction to find their way.

God is the reference point for faith. That has not changed, but it is easily overlooked. Our human inclination is to start with ourselves—our wants and desires. On our own, we cannot change this inclination or reorient our lives. Theologians call this state original sin. But there is good news—God intervened. With the life, death, and resurrection of Jesus, God disrupted our human inclination and offered another way.

Faith is our relationship with God. God created us as relational beings and initiates this relationship with us. God says, "You are mine; I created you. I love you. And nothing changes that." God's love transforms us from objects of creation to subjects of God's love. On our own, we cannot return love to God, but God disrupts our plight and reorients our lives with the gift of grace. Grace is a redemptive gift God gives us to restore our relationship and open us to others; expansive and personal, it frees us to live by a different truth. No one is excluded from this gift. As hard as it is to believe, God's love and grace are boundless.

The love God extends to us is the same love God has extended throughout history; it serves as our reference point. As the first disciples adopted an explorer's mindset and were sent into unknown territory, Jesus said: "A new command I give you: Love one another. As I have loved you, so you must love one another. By this everyone will know that you are my disciples, if you love one another" (John 13:34–35 NIV). Jesus's words are as important to twenty-first-century disciples as they were to first-century disciples. God's love not only transforms us; it also informs how we live.

Loving God and our neighbor orients our journey, and a future where God's love is embodied sets the direction. The future God has promised is a world where peace reigns, creation lives in harmony, and humanity loves freely. We see glimpses of God's promised future every day whenever people of faith join God in loving the world. As new life is cultivated, estranged relationships are reconciled, the lonely are befriended, and good is celebrated, God's vision becomes visible. God invites us to be co-creators of the future and commissions us to be agents of God's love in the world. God's promised future directs our journey of faith, informing how we love God and those around us.

Jesus Navigating the Wilderness

Jesus knew what it was like navigating the wilderness. Right after he was baptized, Jesus spent forty days with God in the wilderness (Luke 4). What can Jesus's experience teach us?

First, *wilderness environments are unruly.* They are remote and uncivilized. Alongside their natural beauty looms danger and uncertainty. While the details of the challenges Jesus encountered are vague,[2] the fact that this story takes place in the wilderness should not go unnoticed. There are many challenges in the wilderness and few inhabitants; as a result, Jesus experienced a range of emotions, just as you and I would. Jesus was the Son of God, but Jesus was also fully human. Recognizing Jesus's humanity and the wilderness context are essential to this story. Alone, hungry, and isolated, Jesus navigated the challenges of the wilderness for forty days. A life of faith will include time in the wilderness.

> Identify a wilderness period in your life. What was it like being isolated in untamed territory? Did you ever feel uncertain and/or out of control? What brought you into the wilderness, and what sustained you? What difference does it make knowing Jesus experienced wilderness times?

Second, *the Spirit led Jesus into the wilderness*. Just as God led the Israelites into the desert, the Spirit also led Jesus into the wilderness (Luke 4:1). Wilderness periods can be of our own making or the result of brokenness in society, but this text notes God led Jesus into the wilderness. Reframing wilderness experiences as initiated by God widens our imagination about God's activity during such times.

The Israelites spent forty years in the wilderness before entering the promised land. This time formed them as a people before they became a nation. Jesus's time in the wilderness formed him for announcing the kingdom of God. Both wilderness periods prepared them for God-sized missions. Jesus and the Israelites left the wilderness different from when they entered. God uses time in the wilderness for God's purpose.

> Has God led you into the wilderness? How did you know it was God? Read the full story of Jesus in the wilderness in Luke 4:1–13. Reflect on why God led Jesus into the wilderness. What was significant about Jesus's time there? What insights does this story offer you?

Third, *wilderness periods are formative*. God used the wilderness to prepare the Israelites and Jesus for the mission ahead of them. For the Israelites, this formation centered on living out God's commands. For Jesus, formation centered on deepening his identity as the Son of God. The Israelites developed practices that embedded the commandments into their daily living. Jesus's time was spent primarily in prayer. Tending our relationship with God and developing practices for daily living are critical to formation.

Jesus's formation also included testing. Hungry and alone, the devil challenged Jesus's human and divine identity. First Jesus was invited to turn stones into bread. Bread, a staple of life, was something Jesus had not had for forty days, and it was a metaphor he later used for his life.[3] But Jesus refused, knowing it was not the time or place. Two more times the devil tested Jesus, and two more times Jesus refused. In the wilderness, Jesus learned to be patient and wait for God's timing. Testing and prayer made it possible for Jesus to know who and whose he was. Jesus's identity was strengthened and internalized in the wilderness, reminding us formation includes identity work.

> How have you been formed in the wilderness? How did the experience change you? What temptations did you face? What guided you?

Finally, *wilderness times create opportunities to look backward and forward.* Jesus's wilderness experience connected to the Israelites' experience in the wilderness; the gospel writers make that connection clear. Our wilderness experiences may not feel connected to God's people in the past, but reflecting on how God has been present throughout history can help us understand God's presence today.

Jesus's story also points to the future. The three temptations foreshadow Jesus's role in salvation. Each temptation—bread of life, announcing the kingdom of God, and victory over death—points to an aspect of Jesus's mission. The devil was keenly aware of God's promises to the Israelites; he knew the Israelites were waiting for a messiah and tested Jesus around those specific characteristics. This story connects with the past and points to what is to come. Wilderness experiences can help us see God's actions in the past and foreshadow the future.

> How have wilderness times connected you to God's past actions? How have they helped you see God's calling for the future? Have you ever had to wait for the right time and place? What was that like?

Wilderness journeys disrupt and stretch; they also open and refine. Times in the wilderness change us. Sometimes we are led by God into unknown territory to prepare us for God-sized missions; sometimes, life circumstances place us there. Either way, God promises to be present, and formation will occur. Embracing our relationship with God while in the wilderness makes such times fruitful for our becoming journey.

Wilderness journeys disrupt and stretch; they also open and refine.

Time In-Between

In 2002, after sixteen years at Prince of Peace Church, I resigned from my job to prepare for a PhD program. It was a time in-between—a time of disruption and new possibilities. Leaving what was and anticipating what was to come, I needed time and space. Prince of Peace was my first full-time job; I had started in youth ministry and ended directing a nonprofit. During my tenure, this dynamic congregation grew from 3,500 to 8,000 members. I thrived in its energetic environment, but I was tired and ready for something new. It was time to step into the wilderness.

During this transition, our family spent the summer in the Dominican Republic launching a Christian school. Our girls, having just finished first and fourth grades, were excited for the adventure. It was a good time for my husband, who had a new role as Director of Missions at our church. And this time in-between made it right for me as well. With high hopes and our belongings packed, we boarded a plane at sunrise in Minneapolis and started our adventure in Jarabacoa before nightfall.

Life in the Dominican Republic was hard, and every day was an adventure. Each morning started with a cold shower and walking to school. The work of starting a school occupied our days, and nights were filled with conversations and household chores. Electricity was unreliable, cell phones a luxury, and weather often disrupted our plans. Yet, overall our family navigated the adventure well. Each of us had a role: My husband's accounting background made him a good fit for setting up the school finances; our two daughters were relationship builders, spending their days at day camp making friends with Dominican youth and American counselors. I accompanied Shelby, the sponsorship coordinator, on home visits.

For six weeks, I roamed the countryside visiting the homes of sponsorship families. These visits pushed me out of my comfort zone. Each day, Shelby and I rode her scooter in a different direction to interview parents. Knowing little to no Spanish, I did a lot of listening (to people who spoke little to no English). I often wondered what I contributed and if I should be reassigned. This role tested me, causing me to doubt my competencies and leadership abilities.

I was never reassigned, and at some point, my doubts turned into gratitude. Boarding our flight home, I was different. I had traveled unconventional paths and listened to parents voice their desires for their children. Reflecting back, their stories illuminated the beauty of the Dominican way of life. But that was not all that had changed. My uncertainty had been replaced with joy, having witnessed brothers and sisters in Christ practice their faith using different customs and languages. I discovered freedom in living a simpler lifestyle at a slower pace and was delighted our children developed friendships with people from different cultures and backgrounds. My husband left with a love for the Dominican people and the beginning of a long partnership with Doulos Discovery School. The summer of 2003 was a blessing for our family and an opportunity for me to recalibrate my perspective of the ministry. Forced to let go of the ministry tools I had previously relied on, I learned to trust the Spirit and accompany others in new ways. There was no better way to start a PhD program than to be formed by God's people in the Dominican Republic.

Back to the Basics

The lessons I learned in the Dominican Republic are similar to the lessons Martin Luther wanted the church of his day to learn—it's time to return to the basics. For centuries, the Roman Catholic Church had added layers or conditions to God's love. Some conditions made God's love dependent on human actions. Some layers reversed the order, seeing human actions as more important than God's action. Some layers qualified God's love, claiming God only loves the morally upright who keep the commandments. Whenever our focus moves off God and embracing God's love, it is time to return to the basics and recalibrate. Recalibrating often entails time in the wilderness.

In 1517, Martin Luther believed the church had lost its focus on God. As a pastor, scholar, and teacher, he was troubled with the direction of the church. He decided to ignite a public conversation by posting 95 theses outlining his concerns on the church door. Luther's post did start a dialog, and that dialog turned into a debate that eventually led to Luther and others being excommunicated from the Roman Catholic Church. Suggesting the church recalibrate resulted in Luther navigating the wilderness. His time in the wilderness was personally formative, but it also was formative for the Protestant Church.

Indulgences were Luther's top concern. Indulgences were a way for people to supposedly purchase repentance for their sins and be assured of salvation after they died. But indulgences were a symptom of deeper issues regarding salvation, authority, and humanity's role in faith. Luther used his time in the wilderness to pray, study, and wrestle with his concerns. As Luther returned to the basics, he saw three beliefs as the essence to the Christian faith: grace, faith, and God's word. He believed salvation is grounded in God's grace alone. Nothing we do can save us; God alone saves. Faith, not works, gives access to salvation, and faith is only possible with God's grace. God's word, written and embodied in Christ, is the church's sole authority. These basics of faith are all the church needs to understand a life of faith.[4]

These three beliefs, summarized as grace alone, faith alone, and word alone, are referred to as Luther's three *solas*.

Luther's call to focus on God and return to the basics ignited a movement that became the Protestant Church. His formation in the wilderness shaped generations of Christians. Today, Lutheran Christians use Luther's three *solas* to orient their understanding of the Christian faith. Seeing God's action as primary and our actions as secondary, we are free to imagine different expressions of church and church leadership as we orient faith to this understanding. With God's word accessible to all, Christians can discover for themselves how to express God's love in the world. For centuries, Protestant Christians have been on a journey of discovering what it means to orient our lives around the basics of faith.

GPS for the Journey

Faith is a living relationship with God, a relationship that God initiates and we are invited into. According to Martin Luther, faith "is God's work in us that changes us . . . our hearts, our spirits, our thoughts, and all our powers."[5] Faith is a gift given and received—"a living, bold trust in God's grace."[6] *Transformed* by God's grace and *informed* by God's promised future, faith *forms* us as we live in a mutual relationship with the one who created us and all of creation.

Living in a mutual relationship with creation, we are formed in faith as we encounter God, others, and the world. Oriented by loving God and neighbor and directed toward God's promised future, *faith formation is the process of accompanying people in discovering a Christian way of life in a dynamic world.* Faith formation is not about creating church members or raising model Christians; it "refers to the patterns of being, doing, and thinking that human communities share and to which they assign meaning."[7] Faith formation is about developing a way of life that sees our encounters in the world as vital for our relationship with God and others. Discovering a Christian way of life in today's highly dynamic environment is our journey of becoming.

In today's VUCA world, getting oriented is a never-ending task. With so many facets of the environment in flux, locating ourselves in relationship to where we want to go is a continuous activity. Thomas Friedman observes that people feel "a loss of control and are desperate for navigational help and sense-making"[8] because their capacities to adapt are not adequate for today's rate of change. Comparing navigating today's context with kayaking rapids, he says stability in dynamic environments comes from paddling with the current or working with the disruptive forces. In other words, we must learn to work with today's changing conditions. According to Friedman, adapting to our highly dynamic world requires discovering "dynamic stability."[9] Dynamic stability, a topic expanded on in the next chapter, is similar to finding balance on a boat; it combines establishing a center of gravity and working with the changing conditions. What if congregations could help people cultivate dynamic stability?

A navigational system designed for dynamic stability must be agile and work with fluid environments. GPS technology is an example of such a system. Portable and accessible, it interfaces with other systems to orient and reset direction from anywhere in the world. With the push of a button, information is up-to-date based on current circumstances. Its ability to quickly integrate and simplify multiple sources of information allows travelers to find their way through known and unknown terrain in the midst of changing conditions, recalibrating as needed. Forming faith in complex times needs a system that mirrors the ease and simplicity of GPS.

A Christian way of life has two foundational movements: *gathering* and *scattering*. Gathered in community, we discover our identity as children of God through participating in Christian practices, encountering God's story, and cultivating relationships with other people of faith. Scattered in the world, we participate in God's mission through celebrating difference, naming pain and injustice, and loving and serving others. Any approach to forming faith must take into account the gathering and scattering movements of our lives.

Recognizing the multidimensional nature of faith is also critical to a Christian way of life. Faith, as laid out in this chapter, can be summarized with four commitments: *gift, compass, witness,* and *agent*.

Faith is a gift of love, for it is "by grace you have been saved through faith, and this is not your own doing; it is the gift of God" (Eph 2:8 NRSV). Faith is not something we earn; it can only be given by God. As a gift, faith anchors our lives and transforms us into subjects of God's love. Faith tells us who and whose we are as it ignites our lifelong journey of becoming. Discovering and rediscovering faith as a gift is vital for forming faith.

Faith is a compass that directs our lives. Faith begs us to "live a life worthy of the calling you have received" (Eph 4:1 NIV). As an embodied faith, God's love and promised future guide our actions and relationships. Faith's orienting capacity helps us see God's presence and join God's mission in the world. Discerning our actions in light of God's activity and present circumstances is a part of faith formation.

Faith's orienting capacity helps us see God's presence and join God's mission in the world.

Faith witnesses to a peculiar story—in particular, the life, death, and resurrection of Jesus Christ. Just like the first-century church, we are "assured of this: God has made this Jesus, whom you crucified, both Lord and Messiah" (Acts 2:36 NIV). Christians are formed by this peculiar story, a story that helps our hearts and minds know and deepens our relationship with God. As we confess our belief in the resurrected Christ, we join the apostles in extending faith to future generations. As we share our stories of faith, we witness to God's continued activity in the world. Learning God's story and sharing stories of faith are critical for forming faith.

Faith creates agents of God's love. Faith moves our attention from ourselves to our neighbor. Sent into the world, we are "Christ's ambassadors, as though God were making his appeal through us" (2 Cor 5:20 NIV). Transformed by God's love, we scatter in the world to love others as God loves us. We create, redeem, and sustain life as we employ our gifts in the places we live and dwell. As we love the unlovable, welcome the stranger, feed the hungry, befriend the lonely, expose evil, and mend brokenness, God's promised future breaks in, and we see the world as God does. Discovering how to join God in loving the world is an aspect of faith formation.

Could these four commitments and two movements create dynamic stability for our journey of becoming? Might attending to these movements and commitments be a GPS for discovering a Christian way of life in a dynamic world? I believe they can. As I've stated before, the church needs to recalibrate faith formation in today's highly dynamic world. The old approaches are not as trustworthy as they need to be, and people need help navigating the disruptive forces in their lives. Setting direction and getting oriented are capacities necessary for navigating uncertain conditions. Developing these capacities provides the buoyancy needed to absorb the waves of change of our VUCA environments and embrace God's steadfast love. With God's love and God's promised future to orient and guide us, what is ahead of us on this journey? The next chapter offers a picture of the forces altering our context and the challenges we face.

How did the canoeing adventure on Seagull Lake end? We chose not to panic. The canoe guide and I each stepped back and got reoriented. Where had we come from? Which direction did we want to go? What distinguishing features could we see in the landscape? As we got oriented, it did not take long to discover we were not where we thought we were; we were facing a peninsula, not the bay with the portage. What we thought was north was actually east. Battling the wind with our novice abilities had twisted our sense of direction. Returning to the basics, we worked with our underdeveloped capacities to read our environment and recalibrate. This is how we found the path to our destination. The journey was not smooth or without challenges, but it was adventurous. We went to bed excited for the days ahead.

The Practice of Telling Stories of Faith

As a fourth grader, I was a guest at the confirmation retreat my dad was leading. During the retreat, Dad shared a story: The Friday before Christmas when I was three, my mom and dad went to a Christmas party while my two-year-old brother Scott and I stayed home with a babysitter. When they returned, Scott was sick, so they gave him aspirin and went to bed. The next morning, Scott was worse, so they took him to the hospital. After an exhausting day of tests and waiting, Mom came home while Dad stayed. That night Scott died from Rey's Syndrome. As Dad shared the story, my mind drifted to a memory. It was of a Christmas tree shining in a dark room with my mom crying in the shadows. That was my first memory. While I knew the facts about Scott's death, hearing Dad tell the story that day had a profound impact on me.

Stories have power. Stories bond, inspire, communicate, and teach. They activate both sides of our brain and tap into cognitive, emotional, and kinesthetic dimensions of our lives.

Stories can convey complex truths, integrate ideas into everyday circumstances, and connect unrelated experiences. Stories are capable of challenging attitudes, beliefs, and behaviors and can linger long after the storyteller is gone. All of us have stories to share, and sharing stories is a transformative practice.

What if everyone told their story? Seeking to find out the answer to this question, Dave Isay opened a StoryCorps booth in New York City's Grand Central station. As a journalist, he had seen the transformative power of telling stories, so he decided to develop a platform for ordinary people to tell their own story. The experiment invited people into a space and into a storytelling process while he recorded. People came to tell stories and to listen, and it was a profound experience.[10] Sharing and receiving stories is "an act of generosity and love"[11] and listening to people's stories felt like "walking on holy ground,"[12] Isay said. As a result, he expanded the platform, and now, twelve years later, StoryCorps has recorded more than 100,000 stories of people from all fifty states. They have the largest collection of African American recorded stories, honored the tenth anniversary of the 9/11 terrorist attack, have partnered with educational initiatives, have honored military personnel, have highlighted people with memory loss and in hospice care, and created a series around justice. StoryCorps is fueled by the power of stories.[13]

What if congregations became platforms for curating stories? Mount Zion Temple, a Jewish congregation in St. Paul, Minnesota, started curating stories as part of a strategic planning process three years ago. Aware that people did not know each other, they used storytelling to create community.

Adapting the "Humans of New York" concept, they interviewed a different person each week and published their story on their website. When the planning process was done, the storytelling practice remained.[14]

Sharing stories has been a common practice in the church for centuries. Not only does sharing stories create the conditions for personal conversations and a caring environment; it also is a means of forming faith. Telling stories of faith provides opportunities to reflect on God's presence in our lives, and hearing stories of faith points to God's presence in the world. Storytelling is an accessible and engaging practice that witnesses to God's transformative love in our lives.

Crafting stories is an art available to people with various skill levels. Prompts help communities adopt or expand this practice. Here are three to consider.

First, interview people. StoryCorps uses this method and offers a great starting point.[15] Questions can vary, but be sure to include some about faith, God, and/or religious experiences. Recording interviews, via audio or video, allows people to tell stories in their own voice and play them for various audiences.

Second, tell stories related to a theme. Four themes StoryCorps found to be powerful are: *thank you, I love you, forgive me,* and *I forgive you.*

Third, write a story based on ten pictures from your life. Once people have written them, share both the images and stories.

Sharing stories is also a means of confessing our faith in God. Storytelling was the main avenue for sharing faith in the early church. Without written accounts, verbal witnessing to Jesus's life, death, and resurrection was the only means available. In today's world, witnessing is often associated with legal systems or testifying to an experience. Witnessing to faith does share our experiences of God, but it also includes confessing a belief in something not seen but known to be true.

My brother Scott's death highlights one of my bedrock claims of the Christian faith. Since the age of three, Christmas and death have been fused together for me. Part of my faith journey was wrestling with how death fits into the Christmas narrative. Christmas had to be more than presents or a Norman Rockwell portrait. Opening myself to the grief of Scott's death allowed me to see how God coming to earth to live among us matters. Christmas is connected to Easter, the time when God declared that life is more powerful than death. Dad's story led me to a deeper understanding of Scott's death, and my telling the story about Scott's death helped me discover hope. My life is grounded in the hope of the resurrected Christ. Christians tell stories of life and death, hope and despair, and love and hate so that others may know the extent of God's love and the hope of the resurrection.

The Practice of Dwelling in the Word

Dwell is a verb that means to reside, occupy, linger, remain, or give attention.[16] Dwelling causes us to pause, focus, and be attentive to time, space, ideas, or people. Our homes are dwellings, physical spaces to be. Dwelling on concepts opens space to reflect and imagine. Dwelling in time heightens awareness of what is happening around us. Dwelling is a practice of slowing down and paying attention. In today's age of acceleration, dwelling is a countercultural activity. Twenty-first-century travelers are conditioned to stay on the move and respond quickly; dwelling is therefore a practice twenty-first-century travelers need to develop.

Being in God's word is an important practice for forming faith. Different traditions prefer different practices for being in God's word. Mainline Christian churches engage Scripture primarily through preaching, studying the Bible, and personal devotions. Each of those practices forms faith in a unique way. One practice for engaging the Bible is "dwelling in the word."

In today's age of acceleration, dwelling is a countercultural activity.

Dwelling in the word is centered on listening—to Scripture, God, and others. Through dwelling, or pausing and being present in the moment, participants open themselves to God and God's presence by focusing on a particular biblical text. Related to the ancient practice of *Lectio Divina*—a Latin phrase meaning "divine reading"—this practice invites participants to set aside their agenda and be with God in community.[17] As participants dwell with God, they listen for the Holy Spirit in the text and in others.

The framework holds the structure for the practice, so anyone can lead it. It opens with prayer and reading a biblical text two times (with two different voices if done within a group). After the readings, participants find a partner and share: "What caught your imagination?" and "What question would you like to ask a biblical scholar?" After listening to their partner, people are invited to share with the group what they heard their partner say. The practice ends with prayer.[18]

To develop dwelling in the word as a spiritual practice takes time. To integrate it into your approach to forming faith, here are some things to consider: First, be thoughtful about the biblical text. While there are no right or wrong texts, find ones that align with the occasion and/or the group's purpose. Because this is an exercise of listening, shorter texts are preferred over longer texts. Second, determine how long you will remain in the same text. Remaining on the same text for an extended period of time allows participants to go deep, but changing texts each time provides variety and texture. Third, review the framework each time. While it seems repetitive, hearing the guidelines and questions reminds people of the framework, why each aspect is important, and of the expectations. Fourth, focus on the listening and hearing dimensions of this practice. Over time, participants can forget the importance of listening to their partner. Because listening is an undeveloped skill, it may be hard for some participants (or they may be overly excited about their ideas and may not honor their partner's). And finally, stay curious and open to the Holy Spirit.

Dwelling in the word is not the place to problem-solve, brainstorm, or share biblical knowledge—it is a space for listening, imagining, and being open.

Dwelling in the word is both faithful and disruptive. It is faithful in that it invites participants into God's story and is an extension of Christian practices across centuries. It is disruptive in that is slows the pace of life, turns our attention to God, challenges assumptions, and pushes us out of our comfort zone. It is a practice that makes room for the Holy Spirit to move in and through us. As communities practice dwelling in the word, it can become a habit that has the power to disrupt and transform previous patterns[19] by redirecting focus from ourselves to God. Pat Taylor Ellison of Church Innovation describes the fruit of this practice. Dwelling in the word

> forms a community of the Holy Spirit, where the Spirit is as welcome and expected a presence as any of the human beings in the group. It gives people the chance to be listened into free speech. It gives everyone a more equitable access into the conversation and the community that is being formed in the scriptural story. And, over time, it gives the group the chance to see that they are living a story, and that their story is a part of God's story. It is not magic or formulaic or prescriptive. It is holy. It creates the community of good will that opens time and space for spiritual discernment for the sake of God's mission.[20]

Activities

1. *Sharing Personal Experiences of Faith Formation*—Invite group members to share about their faith formation experiences by answering three questions from the list below. Give people a few minutes to reflect on their answers, and then have each participant share. (If the group is large, break into small groups.) As people share, practice listening. After everyone has shared, have the group reflect on what they learned.

   Questions:

   What is your first memory of faith and/or church?

   Who were the primary people of faith in your life when you were younger, and what impact did they have on you?

   What was your most memorable experience of faith formation?

   How would you describe the role faith had in your life as a child?

   If you attended VBS or camp, what was it like?

   What has your experience of Christian education been?

   What is one memory of confirmation?

   What role did faith play in a meaningful wedding or funeral experience?

   What has been your worst experience with church?

   How did denominational affiliation impact your faith formation?

How did encounters with other religious groups impact your faith?

In what ways has faith and/or religion been a tension in a personal relationship?

2. *Writing Personal Stories of Faith*—Have people write their story of faith with the following guide: Good stories have a plot, cast of characters, and particular point of view. Using those three elements, think about your own story. What would the plot of your faith journey be? Sum it up in a sentence or concept. Expand it into a paragraph by adding details, context, and descriptors. Make a list of key events. (Events might include a personal revelation, milestone, learning or a-ha moment, and/or crisis.) Add key characters to the list. (Need help? Take five minutes and list all the people who have impacted your faith. Review the list and circle the people most influential related to the plot you identified.) Next, ask yourself what point of view you will take. (You can tell the story chronologically or as your eighty-year-old self, reflecting back on your life. The narrator could be your best friend, or you could limit the story to one key event.) Once those steps are done, sit down and write four to five pages about your life.

   When the stories are done, host a storytelling event. It could be at the church, in a public space, or in someone's home. It could have a theme, be intergenerational, take place during Lent, be the purpose of a retreat, or be the focus for one age group (e.g., for senior adults).

3. *Thinking about Faith Formation*—What is your understanding of faith? How does it align with what was presented in this chapter? Gather a group of people and have them share one concept they appreciated from this chapter and one concept they disagreed with or wanted more information about. Then have people lift up what they think the key concepts of faith and faith formation are. Capture these concepts and have the group compare this understanding of faith with the understanding of faith that they had growing up and/or that they experience in this congregation. Conclude by reflecting on the key learnings that surfaced in the discussion.
4. *Articulate an Understanding of Faith Formation for Your Context*—This activity is a way for congregations to articulate their own understanding of faith and faith formation. If your group completed the ministry audit in chapter 1, this is a great follow-up activity.
   a. *Part 1*—Imagine someone who was not raised in a Christian home and has no understanding of the Christian faith participating in one of this congregation's ministries. What impression would that person have of faith? What would you like to communicate to that person? Who are three or four people who could accompany them in their journey of faith? Then look at your list of faith formation ministries to see what opportunities exist for these groups. What, if anything, is missing?

b. *Part 2*—Think about why faith formation is important to the ministry of this congregation from multiple angles. As a pastor (or staff), parent (or guardian), or participant, what is your understanding of faith and faith formation? What hopes do you have for forming faith? Taking into account the answers to these questions and what you discovered in part 1 of this activity, draft a definition of faith and faith formation for this congregation. Do your best to use language people of all ages can understand. (If you want a process for doing this, move to part 3.)

c. *Part 3*—Give each person a pen and piece of paper. Give people two minutes to write as many words as they can related to the word *faith*. Then have them pair up with another person and create a list of ten words that describe *faith* based on each of their lists. Once the pairs are done, have each pair find another pair (creating groups of four) and create a paragraph describing their understanding of faith based on the two lists. Have each group share their understanding of faith and integrate all of them into one statement. If time allows, compare the definitions with the findings from reviewing the materials from your congregation. Note places of alignment and disconnect.

3

Discerning the Trail: On the Way

The future of the church is dependent upon the hospitality of the world.[1]

It was August, time for our family's annual BWCA canoe trip with our dear friends. We found the entry point to that year's route without a problem. Our rented canoes rested alongside the shore. As veterans, we wasted no time transferring the Duluth packs to the canoes, and after one last visit to the outhouse, we were ready to go. The lake was calling.

As the canoes pushed away from shore and the paddles touched the water, my breathing slowed. It was a lovely day, the kind Minnesotans dream about all winter. Temperatures were in the 70s, the sun was shining, and the water reflected the bright blue of the sky. Our friend Al spoke into the silence with a warning he had received from another camper before we took off. "The bears are out," they had told him. "Make sure your food is hung." We had a new food barrel, so we weren't worried, and we headed toward our first portage.

The first portage was not smooth, but we were in no rush. After lunch and a swim, we headed out again. Each canoe took turns leading songs or sharing stories, and soon we were at our campsite on top of a rocky peninsula overlooking the lake. After our tents were set up, people fished, gathered wood, journaled, and made dinner. By the time we sat down to eat, the hustle and bustle of the city was a distant memory. Everyone was soaking in the beauty of God's country.

Before dark, we washed dishes and made sure our campsite was clean. Al and my husband found a place for the food barrel as the rest of us brushed our teeth and prepared for bed. As we settled in for the night, my husband and I heard a noise. The boys in the nearby tent called for their dad. As Al made his way to them, there was movement in the woods. He looked over and saw something move. It was a bear. Al tried to scare the bear away but had no luck. The bear had his eye on the prize: the food barrel. Within minutes, the barrel was open, and the bear was feasting.

From that point on, the details are blurry. Al and my husband stood guard as the bear ate our food. The boys settled into their tent, and the girls and I tried to fall asleep. It was hours before my mind calmed and I was able to rest. The bear had disrupted our adventure, and I was unsure what the morning would bring.

The Church's Unraveling

Camping trips are not the only thing being disrupted these days. The Christian church in North America is also being disrupted as it unravels from societal norms, values, and practices. This unfamiliar territory is what Douglas John Hall calls the disestablishment of Christianity.[2] Christianity, in the West and many other parts of the world, has been enmeshed within national and political systems. Intertwined with the dominant culture, the church has grown accustomed to a privileged place in society and to operating in concert with established powers. While the Protestant Church has the potential for a disestablished expression of Christianity, most Protestant churches expect society to support faith and its formation. If the church is going to accompany people in discovering a Christian way of life in the twenty-first century, it must embrace the unraveling of the church from the dominant culture and find another way.

Discovering a Christian way of life in dynamic environments requires more than setting the direction and getting oriented; it also requires *discerning the trail*. For the church to discern the trail, it must be clear about its identity and reimagine its relationship with the world. The Christian church's identity stems from a peculiar series of events—the life, death, and resurrection of Jesus Christ. In Jesus, God saved the world from within it, not outside it. As people who live post-resurrection, the cross is more than a one-time event. It is an invitation into "an alternative tradition, gospel, and lifestyle."[3] The cross provides the church its identity.

The cross also defines the church's relationship with the world. God loves the world, and Jesus came and lived among us knowing the world is filled with love, joy, and mercy *as well as* injustice, hate, and sin. Filled with compassion, God came and suffered with us. Compassion is "the highest possible degree of identity with the other."[4] This, according to Martin Luther, is the essence of God.[5] God meets us not outside the world but within it—in our relationships and everyday encounters. Moved by God's compassion, the church lives in solidarity with the world by following "the crucified God into the heart of the world's darkness."[6] Embracing God's expansive love, the church sees all people and places as God's, even the seemingly godforsaken ones. Living between the cross and God's promised future, the church participates in the unfolding of God's kingdom on earth by accompanying others and living in solidarity with the world.

The cross also defines the church's relationship with the world.

Faith provides meaning and gives us courage to face the world's brokenness and enter deeply into the lives of others. Douglas John Hall says, "The whole purpose of faith is to free us for life . . . and to illumine the meaning of what occurs to us."[7] Being present and accompanying others in good and bad times manifests God's love in the world. Discerning *What is God up to?* and *Where can we join?* allows faith to become a plumb line for everyday living. As we face cancer diagnoses, miscarriages, or mass shootings, we let faith guide our actions and provide meaning. As we celebrate wedding anniversaries, sobriety milestones, or adopting a child, we remember faith frees us to live abundantly with others. God's creative and redemptive love is revealed in life *and* death, hope *and* despair, joy *and* sorrow. Our faith comes alive as we discover the lifestyle offered by the cross within our particular circumstances and responsibilities. It is the messiness of the world, which is not yet as God intends, and our current realities that keep faith from being abstract. The particularities of our lives remind us of the relational nature of faith and the complexities of our world. As the church names the peculiar nature of faith and engages the particularities of people's lives, it accompanies people in discovering a Christian way of life and discerning the trail forward.

In the World, but Not of It

For the church to accompany people in discovering the lifestyle offered by the cross, it has to move out of its buildings and into the world. Sent into the world, the church must put aside institutional and societal power, become vulnerable, and be present. Just like God took on flesh "and moved into the neighborhood" (John 1:14, *The Message*), so too must the church move into the particulars of today's messy, disruptive world and discern what God is up to.

It has already been established that the context in which we are forming faith is highly dynamic, and the trail is discerned on the way. Moving into the world begins with listening and gaining a deeper understanding of current circumstances. Using the lens of forming faith offered in the previous chapter, this chapter begins this listening process by addressing five disruptive forces with the goal to help the church rethink how it accompanies people in discovering a Christian way of life. Each disruptive force challenges previous norms and behaviors, as well as provides opportunities and possibilities. This chapter notes how five forces—consumerism, the Digital Revolution, the Information Age, globalization, and religious pluralism—are challenging the church.

Consumerism

Consumerism defines our way of life. It is the water in which we swim, yet few notice the impact it has. Consumerism is an ideology that emerged out of a capitalistic economic system that is built on consumption. For capitalism to work, people must continually consume beyond their need. Mass production, standardization, shortening product life span, advertising, and a fashion market fuel this way of life. Consumerism defines subcultures, motivates political and economic policies, influences social status and business relations, and cultivates a global understanding of "the good life."

Consumerism has disrupted our way of life as commodity logic has turned ordinary items and experiences into objects of capitalistic exchange. Creating an ever-changing vision of "the good life," commodities have moved to the foreground as relationships are pushed into the background, and consuming has become the right and proper thing to do. Without recognizing it, our perspective on life shifted from a *being* existence to a *having* existence.[8]

As consumerism became integrated into all aspects of life, our view of being human began to change. Sociologist of religion Christian Smith says, "Mass-consumer capitalism constitutes the human self . . . as an *individual, autonomous, rational, self-seeking, cost-benefit-calculating consumer*."[9] Socialized into this way of life, our lifestyle is created by negotiating capitalistic systems and accumulating commodities toward a fluid vision of a market-driven ideal. This logic merges consumer choices with identity and makes "satiating one's self-defined felt needs and desires" life's ultimate purpose.[10] This distorted view erodes the gift of being human. Practical theologian Joyce Mercer recognizes that "consumption dominates social practices, such that relationships, activities, space, work, and leisure come to be structured around various practices related to consumption."[11] She goes on to say that within this lifestyle, our relationships, social solidarity, status, and identity are achieved by consumption.[12] As a way of life, consumerism has reframed our understanding of ourselves and our relationships.

Consumerism has now evolved to the point that appearance is replacing accumulation. People ascribe value to "that which 'seems like' the real thing, substituting images, or replications for the thing itself."[13] We see this lived out in the effort people go to in recording events, often at the expense of experiencing them in real time. Our lives become a series of images, photoshopped and edited, that strive toward our aspirations, while our ordinary, everyday life takes a back seat. As affluence rises, commodity value is connected to cultural perception. Emulation, or imitating people you admire, is now a major contributor to consuming.

> What is God up to here? How is a life shaped by the cross different from consumerism? What is God's image of "the good life"? What possibilities or openings exist in your context for experiencing a different way of life?

Digital Revolution

Three inventions created the conditions for the Digital Revolution: The internet provided a common, accessible transportation system, the microprocessor supplied power, and the cloud allowed devices and data to interact with standardized language. With a system, power, and the ability to interact, the Digital Revolution is changing history as it reframes political concerns, reconfigures economic matters, transforms education, and integrates digital technology into all areas of life.

Every society relies on some form of technology, or means by which information is used, to solve the problems of their day. Each technology has embedded within it assumptions, values, and patterns that normalize and/or bias the ways problems are addressed. When technology is disrupted, so is society. Two areas related to forming faith that have been disrupted by the Digital Revolution are *communication* and *information.*

The Digital Revolution is recalibrating communication, which in turn is changing society. When societies had limited tools and were more geographically rooted, communication took place face-to-face in the same location at the same time. As societies became more mobile, new tools were developed which allowed people to broadcast messages to unlimited audiences in various locations. Today, people communicate on a variety of platforms using a constellation of devices. Communication in the digital age is expansive, portable, instantaneous, and participatory.[14]

The year 2007 altered the character of communication. Prior to 2007, digital technology had a limited role in our personal lives and society. After 2007, digital technology became integrated into all arenas of life, changing the way we create, collaborate, think, and live. So what happened in 2007? The most obvious answer is the iPhone, but this is only part of it. In addition, Facebook expanded beyond college campuses, Twitter became its own platform, Google bought YouTube and launched Android, Amazon released Kindle, the internet crossed one billion users, and IBM began creating a cognitive computer called Watson. Each innovation left its mark on society and contributed to the Digital Revolution; together, they changed the character of how we communicate.[15]

Digital technology has decentralized and diversified the means, methods, and patterns people use to communicate. With accessible, easy-to-use digital tools available at little or no cost, long-standing communication methods have been displaced. The communication methods many of us relied on (face-to-face conversations, phone calls, and snail mail) have lost their privileged place as email, Facebook, Twitter, Snapchat, Instagram, FaceTime, Zoom, GoToMeeting, and YouTube gain traction. With today's diversified open market, communication companies are creating new platforms tailored for specific purposes and/or audiences. As a result, our role in communication has changed; we are now directors of our own communication. Communicating effectively in this digital age takes time, as we work across multiple channels, stay abreast of the latest methods and tools, and learn new platforms. The days of being a passive communicator are over. Communicating in this digital age requires active participation in a diverse, decentralized network.

Communicating in this digital age requires active participation in a diverse, decentralized network.

Our active participation takes place in two worlds. As the internet "created a new ecosystem,"[16] a virtual world emerged that welcomes anyone with access and exists whether we show up or not. Integrated, instantaneous, and international, the internet not only disrupted communication, it also complexified it. We now shop, learn, bank, keep up with friends, exchange goods and services, follow sports, and plan vacations online as well as in person. The virtual world is a gift in many ways, yet it also has a shadow side. As a bottom-up ecology, regulating behavior is the responsibility of everyone. It is not guided by policies and regulatory agencies. Relationships now have the ability to be disembodied, and this new reality is impacting our communal life. While the full impact of living in dual worlds is not known, we do know there is no going back in time.

Communication is a social activity, and social media technology provides digital pathways for existing and new social networks to do what we have always done. Prior to 2007, organizations were the primary means for cultivating relationships and solving problems. Post-2007, people have the means for doing this work without organizations. As the number of digital platforms increases, users have a plethora of means for organizing themselves and working for the common good. Social media specialists Jamie Notter and Maddie Grant claim, "One of the reasons social media has grown so fast is that it taps into what we, as human beings, naturally love and need and want to do—create, share, connect, and relate."[17] In the twenty-first century, the means and methods for cultivating relationships and solving problems engage both physical and virtual worlds.

Living in two worlds is not only changing our social interactions and how we address problems; it is also changing how we understand ourselves. Researchers Lee Rainie and Barry Wellman discovered that in this digital age, people are less embedded in groups and are "increasingly networked as individuals."[18] This understanding is called "networked individualism"[19] and places individuals as the focal point, not families, work groups, neighborhoods, or friendship circles.[20] Within this view, there is ongoing pressure to create your own network. With looser ties to home communities, relationships are less geographically defined and connections are more diverse. There is gain and loss in the digital age with regard to forming communities, working for the common good, and understanding ourselves. As the church thinks about forming faith in a post-2007 world, it must reflect on the impact these shifts have on our lives. As MIT professor Sherry Turkle says, "Every new technology challenges us, generation after generation, to ask whether it serves our human purposes, something that causes us to reconsider what they are."[21]

> Where might God be present in these shifts? How is our God-given identity distorted and/or nurtured in the midst of these disruptions? What impact do these shifts have on forming Christian communities and relationships with our neighbors? What openings do they provide for accompanying people in making meaning?

Information Age

Information is another area disrupted by the Digital Revolution. Paper—and the advent of letters, pamphlets, and books—laid the groundwork for the expansion of information, but digital technology accelerated it and made information the currency of the Digital Revolution. The Information Age was conceived when the volume of information exploded as technology developed the capacity to digitally transmit information quickly and efficiently.[22] With the amount of information available to us now beyond our comprehension, the Information Age is changing our *view of power* and *the way we learn.*

Information is hard to control in a digital age. It used to be a restricted commodity for primarily personal and/or institutional gain. Within this view, people depended on hierarchical structures to centralize, control, and manage the flow of information. Today, information is accessible and easy to share. Networks, and their relational connections, have become the primary structure for tending the flow of information. This shift in flow is changing society's posture toward information. As digital technology provides networks with multiple and varying platforms, organizations struggle managing information based on hierarchical values. Valuing accessibility, transparency, and openness, the Information Age operates with a different understanding of power.

Our view of power influences our way of seeing the world, who governs, and how work is done, so it is easy to see that operating with two different understandings of power is disruptive. Jeremy Heimans and Henry Timms provide insight into these two views of power present in today's world. Seeing power on a continuum, they call the hierarchical approach *old power* and the network approach *new power*. They describe old power as *currency*—something limited, to guard, distribute carefully, and use wisely—and new power as a *current*—something endless, to share, be generous with, and entrust others with.[23] While society wrestles with the tension between power as currency and current, the new understanding of power is "changing the way everyday people see themselves in relation to institutions, authority, and one another."[24] New power is paving the way to the future.

As new power views become normative, we must recalibrate how we learn. The formula of a master teacher or expert passing information on to a novice has been disrupted. Everyone is now both a teacher and a learner, and learning is not confined to classrooms or formal programs. The world has become our classroom. Because learning is a social enterprise and our personal capacity to process information is limited, communities of learning play a critical role, and networks that curate, translate, and generate knowledge are crucial. For learning to continue to be vital in our lives, it must adapt to this shift.

Learning in the twenty-first century is not only relational; it is also situated in the world. As such, it connects real-world circumstances to what matters to learners, making learning important and urgent. Learning is this way centers on making meaning as it taps into a human need, connects learning to an outside purpose, and creates relational connections. As such, cultivating meaningful learning communities draws together diverse people around a common interest to make a difference in the world.[25] Learning situated in the world is therefore not only necessary for our well-being; it is also necessary for the well-being of future generations. Because the old pathways for learning and meaning-making have been disrupted, communities able to bring people together to address real-world problems and tap into people's felt needs are invaluable in the Information Age.

> How is God active in this turn? What does this disruption have to do with our journey of becoming? How does a theology formed by a cross fit the view of power emerging in this age? What openings can you imagine in your context for cultivating communities of learning?

Globalization

We see every day how "the playing field is being leveled."[26] Capitalism, digital technology, and our information economy are flattening the world as they remove barriers, open communication, and shift power. As ideas and innovation flow around the world at the speed of fiber-optics, another disruptor calls for our attention—globalization.

Living in the twenty-first century makes all of us global citizens. Our purchases have fingerprints from around the world, and our choices impact people we will never meet. At times, the world's interconnectedness is subtle, and at other times, it is obvious and life changing: Coca-Cola is available almost anywhere in the world, even in places where electricity is unreliable and water is undrinkable;[27] Starbucks has locations on six continents and in seventy-six countries[28] and sources beans from nineteen countries to provide customers with a cup of coffee.[29] The world is showing up in our cities, and our neighbors speak a variety of languages. The world is at our fingertips and lives next door.

Globalization is a complex concept without a precise definition. Since 1961, when Webster's Dictionary first included the term,[30] the concept of globalization has adapted to encompass new developments, knowledge, and innovations from economic, social, cultural, political, environmental, and religious arenas. Recent interests in globalization highlight the world's increased connectivity and interdependence. Connected relationally, economically, virtually, and ecologically, our borders are becoming increasingly fluid, and our challenges have both local and global dimensions.

Just like communication, globalization is evolving. Author and political commentator Thomas Friedman suggests globalization has moved through three phases. *Globalization 1.0* was motivated by the search for resources and expansion of national boundaries, embedded with uneven distribution of power and a worldview informed by national agendas.[31] Within the United States, these colonizing efforts destroyed indigenous civilizations, robbed land of its natural beauty, and cultivated dehumanizing behaviors. *Globalization 2.0* was driven by the pursuit of larger market shares and labor with a capitalistic agenda. As multinational corporations grew, an interconnected, integrated global economy emerged.[32] The world's population became more mobile as travel became faster and cheaper, which increased cross-cultural experiences, expanded people's global awareness, and made global relationships possible. While globalization 2.0 had many good attributes, it also tolerated passive approaches to injustice and inequity and did nothing to disrupt an ethnocentric worldview.

Globalization 3.0, our current state, broke open a new perspective by viewing the world as one ecosystem, community, and market.[33] Nobel Prize–winning economist Amartya Sen, in a conversation with Thomas Friedman, describes the move from 2.0 to 3.0 this way:

> "The Berlin Wall was not only a symbol of keeping people inside East Germany—it was a way of preventing a kind of global view of our future. We could not think globally about the world when the Berlin Wall was there. We could not think of the world as a whole." There is a lovely story . . . about a frog that is born in a well and

> stays in the well and lives its entire life in the well. "It has a worldview that consists of the well," he said. "That was what the world was like for many people on the planet before the fall of the Wall. When it fell, it was like the frog in the well was suddenly able to communicate with frogs in all the other wells. . . . If I celebrate the fall of the Wall, it is because I am convinced of how much we can learn from each other. Most knowledge is learning from the other across the border."[34]

Today, everyone has the potential to contribute, connect, collaborate, and compete on a global stage, and this new reality comes with possibilities, problems, consequences, and responsibilities. Globalization 3.0 has disrupted our ethnocentric worldview and brought attention to the interconnectedness of our world.

Globalization has also increased our encounters with diversity. As a country of immigrants, the United States has always had various ethnic groups. Welcoming immigrants and integrating diverse cultures into society have a mixed history in the United States, and as migration patterns change, so does the texture of our ethnic makeup. In the late 1800s and early 1900s, the United States had the highest percentage of immigrant population (14–15 percent), with most coming from European countries. The lowest percentage was between 1970 and 1980 (with 5–6 percent) as refugees and asylum seekers came to this country. After almost a century of decline, immigration rates are again increasing (now 13.5 percent of the population)[35] with people coming primarily from Latin America and Asia.[36] The next two decades show no sign of this trend reversing.[37] If projections are correct, the United States will become a country of "minorities" between 2041 and 2046.[38] We need practices for embracing difference to face the challenge of increased ethnic diversity.

Living well among diverse cultures requires being aware of our own cultural assumptions, values, and practices, as well as being open to learning from and with people different from ourselves. Culture is the invisible system that captures our multifaceted socialization. More than language, food, or clothing, culture embodies "our basic beliefs and values, our sense of who we are, what we should do, what we should hope for, and how we should relate to other people."[39] As a human construct, culture impacts faith as it reflects how we view ourselves and see God in the world. In other words, cultures are a gift, and "cultures are not innocent."[40] Navigating life as global citizens compels us to reflect on the ways culture forms us and to open ourselves to learn from and with other cultural expressions.

Navigating life as global citizens compels us to reflect on the ways culture forms us.

What is God doing in your community? What does loving God and our neighbor entail as global citizens? How might encountering difference expose the self-centeredness of our worldview? What opportunities exist in your context to experience diverse expressions of God's love?

Religious Pluralism

The United States is not only growing diverse culturally but also religiously. Christianity is morphing into an intricate tapestry with various cultural expressions, ethnic influences, and regional characteristics, while at the same time religious life as a whole is becoming more fluid and interconnected. The experiment the United States began with, separating church and state, has made possible the cacophony of various religious expressions we see today. Yet for most of the United States' history, Christianity operated as a de facto partner with the dominant culture, relying on societal power to flourish. As the Christian church unravels from societal norms, values, and practices, it must discover how to be one religion among many.

Religious pluralism embraces the coexistence of multiple religions. Coexisting involves making space for others, cultivating relationships across difference, and finding ways to collaborate so religious traditions can have a public voice and contribute to the common good of society. Negotiating, compromising, and partnering are capacities needed to live out these commitments.

Religious pluralism works when each religion is valued, and differences are not brushed aside. Many principles of religious pluralism are found within the interplay of the various expressions of Christianity—Roman Catholic, mainline Protestant, evangelical Protestant, and Orthodox, to name a few. Within these expressions, there are points of overlap and points of difference. Some expressions operate with an open posture, some are restrictive, and many fall in the middle. Christianity in the

United States has focused primarily on the distinctiveness of each expression. Moving forward, Christian churches will have to discover what unites them and what Christianity offers society in this time in history.

Religious expressions are also becoming more fluid. As Christianity in the United States becomes less denominationally bound and the presence of other religions increases, people of faith are trying to understand how their relationship with God translates into their relationship with their neighbor. This longing is not new. In 1967, Robert Bellah identified within the American landscape *American civil religion,* or a unifying religious thread "appropriated and abstracted from the Judeo-Christian tradition"[41] that "mobilized at a national civic level for purposes of national order, unity, and purpose."[42] American civil religion pulled from the values embedded within these religious traditions and created a common mindset that influenced not only community relationships but also policies and laws. This framework operated in society at a meta-level, above organized religion. While it tapped into aspects of Jewish and Christian faiths, it was not accountable to nor an orthodox expression of either; it was its own distinctive understanding. As religious pluralism expands, American civil religion is stretched beyond its capacity to make meaning.

Studying the role of religion in public life, public policy professor Robert Putnam and political science professor David Campbell found the United States to be "unusually religious, unusually diverse religiously, and yet unusually tolerant"[43]—a rare combination. While religion connected to politics has polarized the country in many ways (a shift that began in the 1950s), overall this polarization has not created overt hostility or led to segregation.[44] The combination of religious diversity and highly devoted followers usually contributes to violence, civil disorder, and even war. Yet within the United States, there is a higher-than-usual tolerance for religious diversity. Putnam and Campbell credit this tolerance to social networks, or the "high degree of inter-religious mingling or 'bridging'"[45] relationships people have. Today, roughly 35–40 percent of Americans have switched religions, half of all marriages are inter-faith, and almost 90 percent of people believe a person "who is not of their religion can go to heaven."[46] Relationships allow people to live graciously with and among people of varying faith traditions.

An example of this took place in October 2018. A shooter opened fire at Tree of Life Synagogue in Pittsburgh, Pennsylvania, during worship shortly after Rabbi Jeffrey Myers began the 9:45 a.m. service.[47] Some people were pulled out of the sanctuary, but eleven people died and six were wounded. The *Washington Post* cites the incident as the nation's deadliest attack on Jews.[48] Yet that is not the end of the story. The following day, political and religious leaders stood in solidarity with their Jewish brothers and sisters as they gathered for a vigil that overflowed with community members. Rabbi Myers recognized the outpouring of love they received from the local and global community as he addressed the assembly: "My cup overflows with love. That's how you defeat hate."[49] Relationships and love are stronger than religious commitments, ideology, difference, and even hate.

To navigate today's religious landscape, sociologist of religion Christian Smith sees Moralistic Therapeutic Deism (MTD)[50] becoming the current "Operative American Religion."[51] While its tenets have loose ties to various religions, it is not an orthodox expression of any of them. MTD is an attempt to make meaning in the midst of relationships with people across the religious spectrum; its function is purely social, "to foster subjective well-being in its believers and to lubricate interpersonal relationships in the local public sphere."[52] Its existence, however, is disrupting organized religion and challenging orthodox religious beliefs.

At one time, organized religion was the plumb line for Christianity, helping people make meaning. Now people are piecing together their own religious understandings by integrating three, often competing frameworks—civil religion, organized religion, and their individual religious experiences. If congregations do not address religious difference in light of traditional Christian beliefs in a way that helps people navigate today's complex religious waters, people will find other paths. Seeing Christianity as one religion among many requires a framework that honors core Christian beliefs while at the same time honoring other religious expressions. Living well with our neighbors and cultivating respectful religious dialog is necessary. Our approaches must be anchored in ancient Christian practices and beliefs, be flexible in the face of contextual changes, and point toward cultivating a world where all people flourish.

How is God impacting your life? What place does Christianity have in an ecology of diverse cultures and religions? How might congregations help everyday Christians cultivate new conversations, collaborations, and partnerships? What opportunities exist in your context to show love to our religiously diverse neighbors?

Learning to Organize Ourselves

Anchored in Christ and living in solidarity with the world, the church finds dynamic stability as it organizes itself around its calling and works with the environment. This capacity to self-organize allows congregations to adapt to changes without losing sight of their core purpose. As an adaptive system, vitality comes as information and resources get to the parts of the system that need it most, and resiliency comes from doing this work over time within diverse circumstances. If the church is going to be vital and resilient, it must develop this capacity to organize itself. For example, to our calling of accompanying people in discovering a Christian way of life, worship, approaches to teaching and learning faith, and mission work must all contribute to that purpose. If our current approaches do not, then it is time to adapt or abandon them. For the church to embody God's

This capacity to self-organize allows congregations to adapt to changes.

solidarity with the world, it must organize itself in a way that can adapt to environmental changes.

The established church has operated as a bounded-set organization.[53] Bounded sets are static systems that focus primarily on boundaries. Bounded-set churches create clear lines between what is in and out. Examples include a congregation that has a clear definition of membership or only allows members who give financially to serve in leadership. Centered sets, on the other hand, are dynamic systems that move people in a shared direction or engage people around a specific mission. Centered-set churches are clear about what unites them and channel their energy based on that. Examples include congregations committed to dwelling in their neighborhood or devoted to people in recovery. In today's environment, establishing clear boundaries is endless, futile work; bounded-set approaches to congregational life are difficult and do not cultivate the capacity to self-organize. Working with a centered-set approach integrates the capacity to self-organize into the DNA of a congregation.

As the greater church discerns the trail through this unraveling, the local church continues doing ministry and accompanying people in navigating the particularities of their lives. Without the luxury of stopping and starting over, congregations develop the capacity to self-organize as they recalibrate ministry on the way. Messy and exploratory in many ways, this shift takes place as congregations are willing to ask hard questions and discontinue previous practices to organize everything they do around sharing the love of God found in Christ and living in solidarity with the world God loves.

Discerning the Trail

Jesus's time on earth was short. He had three years to accomplish his mission and to prepare others to continue the mission. It was a tall order in a short period of time. Jesus answered his call by *discerning the trail on the way*.

Luke's gospel provides a picture of how Jesus prepared others for this mission. After Jesus was baptized, he called his disciples and began teaching and performing miracles. As Jesus's popularity grew, so did the scope of his ministry. So, Jesus invited his disciples to join in the work. In the midst of feeding five thousand people, healing a boy, foretelling his death, and refereeing an argument, Jesus gave the disciples power to cure disease and cast out demons. Jesus's training came with only a few instructions: Take nothing for the journey. Enter a house when you are welcome. Leave when you are not (Luke 9:2–5).

As diligent students, the disciples went, proclaiming the good news and healing the sick. When they returned, Jesus gathered them to hear about their journey, but their gathering was interrupted by a crowd. Rather than dismiss the crowd, Jesus welcomed them and offered a second training. This time, seventy disciples participated, and Jesus sent them out in pairs to the places "he himself intended to go" (Luke 10:1 NRSV). The trainings were the same, but the tone of the second was more urgent, because "the harvest is plentiful, but the laborers are few" (Luke 10:2 NRSV).

This story could give the impression that faith lived in the world is easy, but two themes in Luke 9 suggest otherwise. First, the environment into which they were sent is tense; the context was being disrupted and Jesus knew it. Herod, the Roman ruler, heard about their healing ministry, became suspicious, and wanted to see them (Luke 9:9). Jesus also mentioned, on two different occasions, that he was going to be rejected, be betrayed, suffer, and die. Jesus was popular now, but things were about to change. The path forward was messy, unpredictable, and risky. Recognizing this tension, Jesus offered a warning—that his disciples were being sent out like lambs in the midst of wolves (Luke 10:3). Be aware that the world into which Jesus's followers are sent is often volatile and not welcoming.

The second theme centers on Jesus's identity. Three times Jesus's identity is discussed: Herod wonders about it; Jesus asks the disciples about it; and Peter, James, and John receive a vision about it. Is Jesus a prophet, like Elijah (Luke 9:8, 19, 30)? Is Jesus the Messiah (Luke 9:18–20)? Is Jesus God's Son (Luke 9:35)? Times of tension raise questions about who Jesus really is.

How does this text help us discern the trail? First, *participating in God's unfolding kingdom is discerned on the way.* There is no predetermined path. The mission and training is simple, but discerning the trail happens on the journey in the midst of our particularities. God empowers and God sends. We go and discern. We take nothing with us, stay where we are welcome, and leave when we are not. We will not feel prepared for the journey and will rely on the hospitality of others. Participating in God's mission does not come with a manual; it comes with a command—go into the world. Go proclaim. Go heal. Go to the places God intends to go. Go alone or with others, but go. And once you have gone, return. Huddle up with other sojourners and share your experiences. Then go again. This is the pattern of the Christian life, going and coming, listening and discerning, scattering and gathering.

Second, *discerning on the way happens in the midst of disruptions.* The world is filled with disruptions; it was for the first followers of Jesus and it is for us. But disruptions do not negate our call to go. Jesus did not instruct the disciples to "Go when the coast is clear," or "Go when leaders support you," or "Go after you get a sign." Jesus's instructions are to go. Do not worry about disruptions, for they will always be there. Disruptions are not what make the journey of faith vulnerable. What makes the journey vulnerable is opening our heart and lives to others. As we go, we will encounter hardship, meet brokenness, and accompany the lonely. As we go, our heart will connect with others, and we will be changed. Suffering *with* others and loving with God-like compassion is what makes us vulnerable no matter the circumstances. Knowing who sent us and whose we are provides hope in the midst of despair, joy in times of sorrow, and clarity in uncertain circumstances. This is the way of life offered by the cross.

Suffering *with* others and loving with God-like compassion is what makes us vulnerable.

And third, *taking nothing with us does not mean we go empty handed.* Jesus had a mission. As he embodied God's love, he offered another way, an alternative lifestyle. As he described God's promised future, he invited people to participate in his mission. God does the same for us. The mission is not ours; it is God's. God empowers, sends, and accompanies us on this mission. As we go, we rely on the hospitality of others. Open to our neighbor, God's love finds its ways into the world. Love is not something that can be forced; it can only be received. So go, clinging to God's love, staying wherever you are welcomed, and moving on when you are not. Learn what it means to be a guest. Listen. Be curious. And discover the lifestyle offered by the cross as you participate in God's unfolding kingdom.

Moving Forward

The morning sun shed light onto the chaos we had encountered the night before. Scattered around the campsite were shredded zip-lock bags, teeth marks etched into empty containers, and tattered bags of beef jerky. The peanut butter container was empty. The trail mix was all gone. And the pancake mix was sprinkled all around camp. In a matter of hours, the bear had eaten four days' worth of food.

For the next half hour, we filled the gnawed food barrel with garbage. Pondering breakfast and discerning our next steps, we sent the kids to the lake to collect water. As they went, they started a conversation with the neighboring campers. "Did the bear come through your campsite last night?" they asked.

"Sure did," our kids responded.

"Did it get anything?" they asked.

"Yep. It got into our food barrel and ate all our food. Looks like we will be going home early."

The kids said out loud what the adults were not yet able to see. This year's BWCA trip would be our shortest—one day.

Before we broke down camp, the neighbors offered us pancake mix and trail mix. With bellies full, we decided to savor our last day and canoe a few more lakes. By dinner, we were back to our vehicles, packing up our cars. That night, a friend let us pitch our tents at their cabin. Two great acts of hospitality graced our day.

While that BWCA trip was not the longest or hardest, it was the most memorable. It remains our family's best adventure story. In thirty-six hours, we experienced many aspects of the wilderness. We soaked in the beauty, drank the cool water, relied on group members, were reminded of nature's untamable forces, and accepted help from strangers. Wilderness journeys are messy and unpredictable. Calm environments can change quickly. Discerning the trail requires not only the skills of setting direction and getting oriented, but also being able to self-organize. In the wilderness, we have to work *with* the environment. On this BWCA trip, nature's disruptive force chased us out of the wilderness, as we did not have the ability to adapt. Yet other times, we've recalibrated, discovering new capacities within ourselves and new perspectives on God and God's world. A life of faith is an unfolding journey within an ever-changing environment. This is no clear path; the trail is always discerned on the way.

Practice of Dwelling in the World

Faith is meant to be lived in the real world, and Christians make the bold assertion that God is active and present in our midst. Therefore, discovering a Christian way of life includes developing the capacity to see God all around us. Christians expect God to show up in our gatherings together, but what about when we are scattered? Dwelling in the world is a spiritual practice that attends to God's presence in the world. The purpose of this practice is to increase our attentiveness to God in our everyday encounters.

Dwelling in the *world* is similar to dwelling in the *word*, as it creates space for pausing and listening to God. Just as God came to earth in the flesh through Jesus, God comes to us through our neighbor. Listening to others and wondering what God is up to are key for this practice.

The practice begins by choosing a focal point that provides a lens to the world. The focal point can be a location (such as a park or shopping mall) or an artifact (such as a newspaper or song). Invite God to be present as you quiet yourself and offer a prayer. Then spend five to ten minutes listening, reading, and/or observing the focal point, wondering, "Where do I sense God's presence?" and "Why?" Spend another five to ten minutes reflecting on how you sensed God's presence. Share your reflections with the group and then close in prayer.

This practice is simple and flexible. It can be done at a gathering at church or in the world. As the practice becomes more familiar, get creative and ask other people to lead. Variations of this practice include:

- Sitting outside your church building;
- Dwelling on the news (TV, newspaper, or web) for several consecutive days;
- Visiting an area school;
- Dwelling on your social media feed;
- Observing interactions at a YMCA (or fitness center);
- Having a teen share a song and why it is meaningful; and
- Watching a popular TV show.

Just as workouts develop physical capacity and create muscle memory, spiritual practices develop spiritual capacities and create spiritual memory. This practice develops three "spiritual muscles." The first is *our understanding of God*. Knowing about God and seeing God in the world are two different things. Some of us know how God is active in Scripture, but we struggle to see God's activity in the world and our everyday lives. Dwelling in the world forms and expands our understanding of God as it moves us between what we know in our head and what we see in the world.

The second is *our view of the world*. Psychologists recognize that our perspective influences our interpretation of life. In this practice, our lens for interpreting becomes visible. Being forced to articulate our experience through our understanding of God helps us more fully see and understand our own interpretive lenses.

The third spiritual muscle is *our imagination*. God is bigger than our comprehension, so stepping outside what we know and opening ourselves to the mystery of God is important. This part of the practice can be challenging, so creating a safe environment with minimal risk and the greatest potential for growth is critical.

Faith is lived in a world that is not yet as God intends it to be. Oriented by God's love toward God's promised future, we live in-between. Discerning what is of God and what is not of God is an ongoing process. The practices of dwelling in God's word and dwelling in God's world independently and together shape discernment. Dwelling in God's word allows God's love to form us. Dwelling in the world awakens us to God's unfolding kingdom around us. Theologian Karl Barth invites Christians to think of a life of faith with the Bible in one hand and the newspaper in the other.[54] This image places our understandings of God directly in conversation with the particular issues and concerns of the day.

Congregational approaches to faith formation usually use God's word as the starting point. Clearly God's word is critical to a life of faith, yet many of these approaches leave our relationship with God detached and distant from our lived experience. A contextual approach to forming faith not only believes faith is to be lived in the world, but sees that God is active around us and that questions of faith are worth exploring. Dwelling in the world offers a practice for discovering God's activity in the world and developing our curiosity. Being attuned to the questions and concerns of our lives helps us discern the trail of our faith journey. As we dwell in, listen to, and become curious about the world, a type of "faith formation curriculum" emerges for congregations to accompany people in discovering a Christian way of life in this time and in their place. Within the particulars of life—our dysfunctional relationships, unexpected tragedies, and moments of joy—opportunities arise for learning about God, ourselves, and our neighbor.

We are peculiar people formed by a God of compassion who dwells among us. Living *in* the world but *not being defined by it,* we engage the world while at the same time imagining more than we can see. Developing this capacity to observe and reflect helps us wonder what God is doing among us as we are scattered in the world and gathered in community.

Practice of Being Hosted

I would rather host than be a guest. As a planner with the gift of hospitality, I love preparing for events, mingling and hearing other people's stories, and knowing people had a good time. I am wired to be a host. Being a host is comfortable. Hosts choose the food, decide the time, and create the atmosphere. Being a guest is vulnerable. I recently had dinner at a new friend's house. It was his Sabbath meal, a meal with special meaning, and I was honored to be invited. And I panicked, unsure how to be a good guest. What do I wear? Do I bring wine or flowers? What is the appropriate time to arrive? Given my diet, will I be able to eat the food?

> Embracing the role of guest requires pushing aside expectations, trying new things, and trusting others.

Over the years, I have discovered patterns of hospitality and practiced being hosted. In the Dominican Republic, I learned to navigate different cultural norms. As a guest in other faith communities, I appreciated the guides who accompanied me. When I volunteered at a school, the children's smiles and staff conversations made me feel welcomed. Embracing the role of guest requires pushing aside expectations, trying new things, and trusting others. It demands we show up emotionally as well as physically. It forces us to discern when to make our needs known and when to go with the flow. Being a good guest involves being curious, generous, and humble.

Hospitality is a prominent theme in Scripture. Welcoming the stranger is an Old Testament mandate. It was one way the Israelites remembered their time enslaved in Egypt[55] and how they cared for travelers.[56] Jesus relied on being hosted all of his adult life and frequently taught about hospitality. Jesus accepted the gift of an unexpected guest at dinner (Luke 7:36–50) and was served by a Samaritan woman at a well (John 4:1–42), Jesus talked about the importance of being present with Mary and Martha (Luke 10:38–42) and demonstrated that he operated with a theology of abundance in feeding five thousand people (Luke 9:10–17). Receiving and giving hospitality are spiritual practices for followers of Jesus.

Being a guest is risky; it means living with hands open to the world. Living that way is hard, at least for me. My friend Dawn expanded my imagination about living with such a posture. As an actress, she worked in various locations around the country; for four full years, she leaned into the practice of being hosted. Dawn decided to let go of her lease, placed her belongings in storage, and relied on the hospitality of others. Based out of New York, she used her network to let people know she was looking for short-term places to stay. And guess what? People opened their homes to her. As time went on, she expanded her network and new opportunities presented themselves. As she told me about her experiment, I became anxious. I had a need for the security (imagined or real) of a stable address. Without a long-term plan, I became uneasy. Yet this posture of living with our hands open to the world is exactly what Jesus is inviting us to embrace. Through conversations with my friend, I was challenged to rethink what being hosted really means.

Lydia Place is a ministry which is teaching me what it means to be hosted. As a missional community in St. Paul, Minnesota, the people of Lydia Place are committed to being in and for their neighborhood, living with hands open. As they discern how to be present within existing structures and activities, they are continually asking, "What is God up to?" and "Where are we being invited to join?" This ministry began as the pastor walked the neighborhood and created relationships with business owners and area leaders. It matured as relationships deepened and expanded. Today, they worship weekly in an art gallery and lead a communion worship at an apartment complex. But worship is not the center of this ministry. Equally important is their participation in the neighborhood council and working toward food sustainability. Lydia Place has grounded its ministry in a theology of dwelling in the neighborhood with the practice of being hosted.

What if the church is being called to embrace the role of guest? Embracing this role means living with hands open to the world—vulnerable, curious, and humble. Vulnerability entails being a part of the greater community and speaking their language. Curiosity involves eating different food and gathering in new ways. Humility means setting aside assumptions and listening more than speaking. Being hosted focuses on our neighbor. It involves trusting strangers and rethinking presuppositions. God's table is one place to exercise this posture, as all are guests at God's table.

The next time you gather for communion, participate with the mentality of a guest. How does that impact your experience? God's mission operates in the same way. We are invited to join God in loving the world. Good hospitality, as both host and the one hosted, creates an environment where relationships are formed and love can grow. God, in God's infinite wisdom, has chosen to be revealed in communities of hospitality, as we encounter our neighbor on the street and gather around bread and wine.

Activities

1. *Discerning the Trail*—Read Luke 9:1–10:3. Reflect on what this text means for today's followers of Jesus using the three themes named in this chapter.

   Theme #1—*Participating in God's unfolding kingdom is discerned on the way*. What is your reaction to this theme? What is encouraging and what makes you uneasy?

Theme #2—*Discerning the trail happens in the midst of disruptions*. This theme highlights the vulnerability in participating in God's mission. How have you experienced vulnerability as a result of your faith? Why is it important to be aware of this?

Theme #3—*Taking nothing with us does not mean we go empty handed*. What helps you integrate faith into your life? How does your relationship with God help you in disruptive times?

2. *Practice Being Hosted*—Review the practice of being hosted and do a few experiments. Find several people to join you. After the experiments, reflect on what they were like, personally and as the group. Here are questions to guide your reflection: What was hardest about being hosted? What surprised you? What was your biggest learning? How did framing being hosted as a spiritual practice impact the experiments?
3. *Reflect on the Five Disruptive Forces in Your Context*—Five disruptive forces were addressed in this chapter. Learning how these forces are shaping your context is vital for tailoring your approach to faith formation. Using a basic environmental scan, have people explore the impact these forces are having in your congregation, city, and/or greater community. Scans can be informal, such as talking with people within your own networks who have different points of view. Scans can also be more strategic and intentional. For example, you may

set up appointments to talk with people who are knowledgeable about areas of interest and/or explore existing research about the area of interest. No matter which approach you use, assign different people areas to investigate. (If you have more than five people, have them work together.) Give people a month to do this work and then gather to share learnings. The questions below are a guide, but feel free to create your own questions.

Consumerism—How have shopping patterns changed in the last five years? What new practices are people using? What changes do you anticipate in the next several years? What is the biggest impact of consumerism in your area? What trends in consumption do you see? How is consumption different across generations? What role does consumption play in people's everyday life?

Digital Revolution—How are digital tools enhancing life for your community? How has communicating changed with the advent of digital tools? How is digital communication impacting relationships in your life and community (e.g., in school or in parenting)? In what ways are digital tools strengthening relationships? What necessary relational capacities are not nurtured with digital tools? What new relational capacities are emerging in this digital age? What is the biggest disruption digital technology has made in your community?

Information Age—Describe how you interact with information today. What new patterns are emerging? What practices have gone away? How do people expect to receive information today? Describe how you learn about something you are interested in (for example, learning a new hobby or solving a current problem). What is the most important capacity young people will need to learn in the future? What role do computers play in solving problems? What role do humans play in solving problems?

Globalization—Describe how your community is connected to other areas of the world. What shifts around diversity has your community experienced? How have organizations within your community responded to these shifts? Share stories that highlight these shifts. What shifts do you anticipate in the future? What work could be done to anticipate those shifts?

Religious Pluralism—How has the religious landscape in your community changed in the last ten years? Compare the role religion played ten years ago with the role it plays today. What role could or should religion play in the next ten years? What would it take for that to happen? How do people's lived experiences with faith align with the established religious organizations in your community? Where do people turn when they have questions about God and religion?

4

People on the Move: #LivingAbundant

> The social fabric is tearing across this country, but everywhere it seems healers are rising up to repair their small piece of it. They are going into hollow places and creating community, building intimate relationships that change lives one by one.[1]

Our Minnesota winter came early that year. By Thanksgiving, the single-digit temperatures made it feel like January. The day after Thanksgiving would have been a nice day to stay inside and make Christmas cookies, but our daughter had an alternative plan—get outside. Our family loves being outside in the summer and fall, but our daughter wanted to

#OptOutside—more on that below—in the winter. So on Black Friday, with the windchill below zero, we prepared to spend the day outside.

If you wanted to challenge societal norms, would *you* choose consumerism's biggest holiday to do an experiment? That's what outdoor-gear store REI did. REI, a purpose-led co-op of sixteen million members, believes "a life outdoors is a life well lived."[2] On Black Friday 2015, they embodied that purpose as they closed their doors (something no other large retailer had done before), paid their employees to be outside, and invited America to join. Participants used the hashtag #OptOutside to share images of their outdoor adventures, and more than 1.4 million people and 170 companies and nonprofit organizations did. It was an experiment that worked. The next year, #OptOutside quadrupled, and now fifteen million people and 700 organizations have "created a new tradition to #OptOutside on Black Friday."[3] REI is advancing their mission and cultivating a vision for living well as they experiment their way into the future.

REI has a long tradition (eighty years) of making great outdoor gear accessible, offering adventure experiences for all abilities, and telling inspiring stories, but REI's mission is not complete until outdoor activity is helping everyone live well. REI is concerned about society's sedentary lifestyle, citing that half of Americans are not doing any sort of outdoor activity.[4] #OptOutside addresses this challenge, as do research and partnering with hundreds of organizations. #OptOutside is not about a day or event; it is about an abundant way of life.[5]

A New Narrative

As I see it, Christian formation is the number one challenge facing the church today. Declining church attendance and an increase in people not claiming any religious affiliation are signs our current approaches to forming faith are not working. What risks will the church take to address this challenge? What experiments will it engage in to witness to future generations? It is time for the church to boldly live its mission and embody a new narrative.

The church is not dying. God is present and active, the Holy Spirit continues to transform, and Christians regularly pray and confess their belief in the triune God. The church is being disrupted. Dying and disrupted are different; death is the absence of life, whereas disruptions happen in the midst of life. Disruptions close paths as they open others, forcing the church to change current patterns and experiment with new forms—but the church is more than patterns and forms. The church is God's, and its future is a gift we receive, not something we create. As God's people dwell, listen, and wait with open hands, minds, and hearts, God shows up. The path to the future is discerning God's presence in the midst of disruptions and the uncertainties of the wilderness.

The future expression of church is not yet apparent, but characteristics are emerging. As I've already said, the church is becoming less established and more fluid. Decentralized and dispersed, it looks and behaves differently than before, functioning more like a network than a hierarchy. The church of the future is agile, with unprecedented collaborations, blurred boundaries, unique communities of learning, and leaders equipped in a constellation of ways. It appears haphazard and chaotic as conventional lines of authority give way to addressing real-world challenges, but the Spirit is at work sparking imagination and bringing forth new voices. God is creating, redeeming, and sustaining life, and we are invited to participate.

While some people want the institutional church to lead the church into the future, the truth is, ordinary people doing extraordinary things have always been the way God's future has entered the world. Transformed by God's love and directed by God's promised future, we are a becoming people. Placed in the world and on the move, we are invited to join God in co-creating the future. Like it or not, God's crazy plan for redeeming the world includes us. Are you ready to lean into this wilderness journey?

Like it or not, God's crazy plan for redeeming the world includes us.

Abundant Life

God has a vision for our future. Revelation 21 offers a picture of that future. Seeing a new heaven and earth, a voice says, "Look! Look! God has moved into the neighborhood, making his home with men and women! They're his people, he's their God. He'll wipe every tear from their eyes. Death is gone for good—tears gone, crying gone, pain gone—all the first order of things gone"

(Revelation 21:3–4, *The Message*). God's vision is a world with no tears, no death, no pain, and God literally living with us. The old is gone, and our home becomes God's home. What can we learn about abundant life from God's vision for our future?

First, *God is about life.* God's first and last moves focus on life,[6] with Christ's resurrection as God's signature on the world. Life is God's powerful creative and redemptive force in the world. God's life force is wired into all living things. God sees potential for life in all aspects of the world, and God wants all of creation to live abundantly. Life, not death, has the final word.

Second, *life with God transforms our existence.* Christ's resurrection offers life after death, but it also transforms life on earth.[7] Baptism marks our transformed existence and offers us practices for living abundantly. As we "live among God's faithful people, . . . hear the Word of God and share in the Lord's Supper, . . . proclaim the good news of God in Christ through word and deed, . . . serve all people following the example of Jesus, and . . . strive for justice and peace in all the world,"[8] we live connected to God, others, and the world. This way of life frames our everyday encounters and guides our witness. Transformed by God's grace, people of faith promote life and resist anything not focused on life.

Third, *abundant life is a foretaste of God's promised future.* While the future God promises will not be fully realized until the end of time, Christians orient their everyday encounters toward God's vision. By striving for justice, serving all people, and sharing the Lord's Supper, people of faith taste God's future now. As hope displaces despair, love overcomes hate, and peace comforts troubled souls, the gap between God's future and the world's present struggle is reduced, and God's people live as if God's future is among us.

Fourth, *abundant life is driven by hope.* Faith reorients time. Revelation 21 is a word of hope for the present, grounded in the past with an eye to the future.[9] It is a reminder of God's faithfulness across time. God is actively creating, sustaining, and reconciling the world, even when we do not see it. This was true for our ancestors, and it is true for us. The world is not yet as God intends, but we can trust God will bring it to completion.[10] Suffering and pain call the future into question, but life is a vigorous force. Hope pulls us toward a future where life is more powerful than death. God's grace and love fuel abundant life, sending us into the world with the capacity to see beyond current circumstances.

The Christian life is framed by a theology of abundance. Abundant living allows God's grace and love to continually transform our lives. Martin Luther wanted to live every day in God's abundance, so each morning, he made the sign of the cross on his forehead and prayed for the Holy Spirit to guide his day. A theology of abundance changes how we see ourselves and the world. Because God sees possibilities for life everywhere, we also trust in life's creative and redemptive power. As we join God in creating, sustaining, and redeeming life, we participate in co-creating the future and live abundantly.

A theology of abundance changes how we see ourselves and the world.

Living Particularly

Abundant life is not a utopian lifestyle; it is the by-product of loving God and our neighbor in the ordinary aspects of life. As I said above, Christians are agents of God's love, co-shaping the future. All of us have this same call, but we each live it differently. The ways we push against hate, evil, and death are dictated by the particulars of our lives. Loving our neighbor is not an add-on; it is integrated into everyday living through the particularities of our work, relationships, and context. For example, I love my neighbors in Minnesota as a teacher, author, mother, and friend. The ways I care for students, tend relationships, and approach writing contribute to how I co-shape the future. My friend Dawn loves her neighbors in New York as an actress, coach, business owner, and daughter. As she shares her gifts inside and outside the church, she embodies a vision of God's creativity and encourages people to discover God's unique design for them. My sister-in-law Erin loves her neighbors in California as a pastor, colleague, mother, and healing touch therapist. She embodies grace and works for justice in her official capacities as well as her community involvement. Each of us has different locations, relationships, and roles that situate us differently in the world. God's love moves into the neighborhood through us. Seeing every moment as the possibility for life and love, God's dispersed people are a powerful force in the world.

The theological concept for this idea is vocation. The word *vocation* comes from a Latin word meaning "to call." Long before career counselors or life coaches talked about vocation, Christians used the term to refer to how their everyday lives were made holy. Martin Luther saw vocation as a way to remind people everyone has the same status before God. We all are saved by grace and receive faith as a gift. Vocation also informs how our lives are made holy—by loving our neighbor. For Luther, our stations in life, or particular locations, roles, and responsibilities, are particular avenues for loving our neighbor.

The apostle Paul directed first-century followers to live as the unique, transformed people God called them to be. He said the old ways no longer fit, so "take on an entirely new way of life" (Eph 4:22, *The Message*). Everyone is to build up the body of Christ and work for the common good, but each of us has our own relationships and gifts. These unique gifts, relationships, and experiences have a purpose—to love our neighbors. God does not need our care, but our neighbor does because the world is not yet as God intends. To witness to God's way of life and join God in co-creating the future, we use the particularities of our lives, and our unique gifts, to share God's love.

> How can the concept of vocation inform how you love your neighbor? How are your relationships and roles avenues for creating and sustaining life? How do your stations provide ways for you to be an agent of healing and reconciliation? How is loving others changing you?

#LivingAbundant

The narrative driving people of faith is abundant life. In the midst of today's disruptions, God's people need a vision for living abundantly. Accompanying people in discovering a Christian way of life requires cultivating a vision of abundant life that connects people's everyday lives with God's promised future. Taking cues from #OptOutside, the church could try a bold experiment. Could you close your doors on a Sunday morning and send people searching for abundant life? Stories and images could be captured with a hashtag—#LivingAbundant—to make God's presence in the world visible. Images might include a toddler playing with an elderly man in a nursing home, neighbors working together in a community garden, people of different religions sharing stories over a meal, or white and black neighbors standing alongside each other after a neighborhood shooting. Imagine images and stories flooding social media, creating a narrative of abundant life, giving people a snapshot of God's promised future. God is present in the world and God's people are on the move. What if the church invited people to notice and share their stories?

Learning from the Future

Learning in the twenty-first century is situated in a world where the challenges are complex and disruptive forces are altering the environment. Applying best practices, changing worship styles, or revamping confirmation curriculum do not penetrate deep enough into today's challenges because they were designed for different contexts. In disruptive times, learning must calibrate toward the future. Researcher, author, and innovator C. Otto Scharmer discovered that three elements are necessary to learn from the future: *a framework for seeing blind spots, a process for implementing change,* and *a new operating system.*[11]

Seeing Blind Spots

Learning naturally builds on lessons from the past, so learning from the future "requires us to *suspend* our judgments, *redirect* our attention, *let go* of the past, *lean into the future* that wants to emerge through us, and *let it come.*"[12] Knowledge and wisdom develop as new information and discoveries are integrated into current understandings. Information is accepted or rejected based on those understandings. For example, learning the alphabet and grammar is the foundation for developing vocabulary and writing capacities. Learning a foreign language, with a different alphabet and/or grammar, requires letting go of foundational understandings and assumptions. Over time, knowledge becomes so deeply embedded that we need assistance uncovering and naming our assumptions. Our assumptions create blind spots, so recognizing them is the place to start learning from the future.

For lifelong Christians, recognizing our assumptions about church and forming faith is hard, especially if our experiences have been significant in providing meaning. Try this exercise:

Write down your description of "church." (Examples might include elements of worship, programmatic approaches to ministry, mission outreach, pastoral care, and/or relationships.) Reflect on your experience of church by making two columns: List the ways church has been meaningful to your relationship with God in one column and how it has been an obstacle to your relationship with God in the other column. Then create a list of church expressions. (Examples might include mainline, Pentecostal, mega-church, small-town, urban, evangelical, social justice, etc.) List as many as you can. Review the list and ask yourself how you view each expression. Write down your opinions and/or critiques. As you scan the list, what key assumptions seem to inform your idea of church? Are there assumptions that you might need to change or let go of? How might you do that? Suspending judgment is hard but critical work for learning from the future.

Implementing Change

Learning involves change, and humans have the ability to change. Our past does not predetermine our future. We are not victims of disruptions or enslaved by history. However, for learning to be a gateway to change, it requires more than knowledge; knowledge alone rarely translates into changed behaviors or mindsets. Change requires a process. Therefore, learning from the future includes growing our capacity to implement change.

Change involves emotions and behaviors as well as understanding. Business professor Chip Heath, along with his brother, social entrepreneur Dan Heath, in their best-selling book *Switch*, offer a change process that integrates the head, heart, and environment. The metaphor they use is a person riding an elephant on a path. The rider represents the rational aspects of change, the elephant represents the emotional aspects, and the path represents the situation surrounding the change. Implementing significant change must direct the rider, motivate the elephant, and shape the path.[13] This process involves our hands and hearts as much as our heads. It entails listening to our gut, gathering feedback, and imagining new possibilities.

A congregation eliminating their Sunday morning adult education hour might begin implementing change by identifying the rider. For example, the people most impacted by the change may be a group of senior adults. The change might include piloting a learning series on Tuesday mornings. Motivating the group to change includes not only enticing the group to attend these Tuesday morning sessions, but also dealing with their loss. Tending their grief could include a "funeral" for the current Sunday morning education hour where people share their experiences and name what they will miss. Moving forward might entail a party to launch the pilot. The pilot could include previous speakers as a bridge from the old to the new. The sessions could be in the same room, and some of the senior adults could be hosts who offer feedback to the staff. This process tends to people, emotions, and the situation. Being aware of blind spots and developing capacities for change are critical for the present to become "a gateway to a field of future possibilities"[14] and for us to become co-shapers of the future.

New Operating System

Learning from the future also needs a new operating system. C. Otto Scharmer believes all of us need to "update the mental and structural operating code"[15] by which we live. His research shows most of the world's operating systems are *ego*-centric, or place themselves at the center. Thriving as a diverse interconnected global community requires *eco*-centric operating systems, or placing the good of all at the center. While Scharmer's argument is not theological, his proposal invites us to co-shape a future where everyone lives abundantly. Abundant life relies on an *eco*-centric "mental and structural operating code."

> Thriving as a diverse interconnected global community requires *eco*-centric operating systems.

Operating systems are both critical and invisible. Operating systems tend connections and manage flow. Think about what a computer operating system provides: basic functions, as well as connecting hardware and software (think Windows, Apple's OS, Linux, and/or Android). Computer programs work with the operating system. When these systems work well, users navigate effortlessly, paying no attention to the operating system. When they do not work well, users struggle as inefficiencies become evident. Because computer operating systems are software, they are agile, easily updated to adapt to changes. In the same way, operating systems play a fundamental role in organizations.

Many ministry leaders implement change by revising programs. Using the computer analogy, ministry programs function like computer applications, or apps. Apps work *with* operating systems to carry out their particular functions. Forming faith does require revising ministry programs, but in disruptive times, that is not enough. Learning from the future, the church must also recalibrate its operating system so it can work with today's dynamic environment. Recalibrating operating systems allows congregations to reboot their basic functions and design agile faith formation programs that fit their context. This book provides congregations an upgraded operating system and a guide for custom-designing programs that fit your context.

Because the connections and flow operating systems provide are primarily invisible, today's disruptive forces offer the church a gift. As our relational connections and flow of information are disrupted, assumptions are unearthed, and the church has the opportunity to see its blind spots and open itself to what is emerging. Operating systems oriented to the future that work with dynamic environments are necessary in wilderness times.

Playgrounds of Possibility

What is emerging from the future regarding faith formation? As we suspend our assumptions and recalibrate our operating systems, a distinct model for forming faith has not yet materialized. Therefore, implementing change requires experiments oriented toward the future. Clues for where to begin are surfacing. This section will address five playgrounds of possibility that arise out of the disruptions named in the previous chapter: *reclaiming our relational existence, cultivating community, celebrating diversity, contributing to the common good,* and *being one among many.*

Reclaiming Our Relational Existence

Our relational identity has been disrupted. Identity formation has become intertwined with consuming and/or networked individualism. Identity is now something individuals construct, as consuming morphed our relational existence into an existence of accumulating and emulating. Disconnected from a larger narrative and apart from tradition, identity has developed into a composition of choices related to an ever-changing view of "the good life," and belonging has become conditioned by societal norms. Within a capitalistic system, humans are objects and relationships are a means to an end; values are detached from contexts and ethics are reduced to compassion without consequences. Identity framed by consumerism denies our worth as God's creations, negates our relational character, and curtails our agency.

The relational dimension of identity formation is evolving from geographically bound communities to personalized, me-centered networks. Constructing identity in a digital age involves managing our public persona via a loose social network within two ecosystems. Our public personas are determined by our "desired place in the social order,"[16] and our relational connections are a means for achieving that end. As relationships are tended online and in person, they are more diverse and fluid, with fewer being long-term. As a result, the places we have to exercise our human ability "to love, to care, to hope, to trust, and to build voluntary communities based on shared values"[17] are disappearing. Identity shaped by networked individualism has many of us digitally connected but emotionally isolated. Placing ourselves at the center in a loosely networked community without a communal vision of well-being neglects our human need for deep relationships and distorts our reason for cultivating communities of meaning.

Christians believe identity is given by God. Created in God's image, all human beings are loved and valued by God. God's love is therefore the baseline for our identity, and relationships are the essence of our being. Love bonds relationships and is the source of life; death, according to theologian John Zizioulas, occurs when persons cease to love and be loved.[18] Identity, just like abundant life, is discovered by loving God and our neighbor. As we live our distinct God-given design and connect to other people, we learn what makes us unique, unrepeatable persons. As we love others as God loves us, we discover full, abundant life. Identity is not a nebulous free-floating construct; it is our existence tethered to God's love that unfolds as we relate to God, others, and the world.

Love opens us to others, as love opens God to us. Being open is core to our relational existence and a signature of faith. Making room for others, we form relationships and create community without losing our distinctiveness. As love moves our attention away from ourselves to others, relational connections are transformed from instrumental exchanges into relationships of mutual regard. Love's mutuality is compassion embodied. Christ modeled this type of relationship, something theologian Jürgen Moltmann calls *open friendships.*[19]

Persons are not the same as individuals. Persons are relational beings, whereas individuals are defined apart from relationships. Seeing ourselves as individuals creates the illusion our lives are not connected to others and implies we are not dependent on others.[20] God designed us to be connected, to be persons in relationship. Human beings thrive within a web of relationships where they are known and have deep connections. Sin is what disconnects us from our relationships with God and others. Living detached from others erodes our well-being, destroys community, and obstructs abundant life.

God designed us to be connected, to be persons in relationship.

Christians live by a countercultural claim—namely, that our identity is communal and comes from God. God's vision for our lives comes from this countercultural claim, and it involves loving God and our neighbor. Living in community embraces God's design for our lives and defends our relational existence. As congregations nurture identity as a gift from God and reinforce the relational nature of our personhood, they refute identity as emulation within me-centered, personalized networks and accompany people in cultivating a life of meaning.

Cultivating Community

How we relate to each other has been disrupted. The ways we connect, the type of bonds we have, and how we communicate have been affected by our digital world. Our relational connections are integral for creating "social capital," or the "social networks, norms of reciprocity, mutual assistance, and trustworthiness"[21] within society. Social capital contributes to the common good through bonding (or inward-facing) and bridging (or outward-facing) relationships. Social capital has been declining for years, but recently, social entrepreneurs are reversing the trend. Public policy professor Robert Putnam and nonprofit director Lewis Feldstein studied their efforts and discovered that creating "spaces for recognition, reconnection, conversation, and debate"[22] is vital for social capital. Cultivating social capital is slow, inefficient work but critical for the well-being of humanity.

Communication patterns provide insights into our current relational ties and personal longings. Theologian and professor Andrew Zirschky, in *Beyond the Screen*, believes a basic human need is driving young people's digital media usage—a hunger "for continuous, meaningful relationships of presence."[23] His research challenges us to reflect on how community is cultivated in a digital age. Once, community was defined primarily by geography, such as a neighborhood or city, and relational ties determined by contextual realities. As mobility increased, community was cultivated via hosting or convening, and attendance was the sign of belonging.[24] Today, community is not correlated with geography or physical presence but related to "a sense or feeling of social support."[25]

Congregations make assumptions about the strength of people's relational connections without investigating whether their practices are actually nurturing meaningful relationships. Cultivating intimate relationships and a sense of belonging involves sharing ordinary, mundane aspects of life, not our public personas or "seems like" moments. Exchanging everyday stories and inviting people into the messy parts of life strengthen relational bonds and create intimacy. Congregations that create such opportunities meet people's basic need "to love, to care, to hope, to trust, and to build voluntary communities based on shared values."[26] Connecting regularly and frequently, online or in person, has a profound impact on relationships and exemplifies Luther's understanding of vocation. Relating with others around our stations in life is a natural way to foster intimate relationships and create meaning. The relational connections we make through our roles and responsibilities increase social capital as well as provide opportunities to share God's love. Being present and accompanying each other in daily life are significant acts of love that contribute to society's well-being and create meaningful communities.

Cultivating meaningful relationships is part of the fabric of congregational life. While contributing to social capital is not the primary concern of congregations, nurturing both bonding and bridging relationships is part of our call to love God and our neighbor. As congregations become communities where people practice open friendships and experience strong relational connections, they develop into "spaces for recognition, reconnection, conversation, and debate"[27] and contribute to people flourishing.

There is a biblical model for such communities. The first-century church embodied bonding and bridging relationships as they devoted their lives to the apostles' teaching, praying, sharing meals, selling their possessions, and seeing to each other's needs (Acts 2:42–47). The Greek word for this type of community is *koinonia,* which translates to "communion" or "joint participation." As people are united by God's love and share life together, they embody *koinonia.* Zirschky summons the church to respond to people's longings by becoming *koinonia* communities. To do this, we must expand our capacity to be communities of presence where diverse, distinct persons are present with and for one another. Congregations are uniquely positioned to live this way because they are united and empowered by the Holy Spirit. *Koinonia* is a biblically based alternative to networked individualism that informs our communal gatherings and guides our scattered lives.[28]

In holy communion, we get another picture of Christian community. At this meal, God sets the table and unites those gathered. As God transforms bread and wine, God becomes present and the radical inclusivity of God's love is made known. As followers of Christ eat this meal, they remember Jesus's life, death, and resurrection and taste God's sacrificial love. Aware of the need for reconciliation and healing, people reconnect with God and are renewed to love their neighbor. At God's table, we see beyond the present and remember that the path to God's promised future involves dying to ourselves and being open to God and our neighbor. Congregations become communities of presence as they remember that God is the host.

Cultivating community not only adds value to people's lives and enhances social capital; it also creates a holding environment for forming faith. Bonding and bridging relationships are crucial for accompanying people in discovering a Christian way of life in the world. Creating relational ties around the ordinary, mundane aspects of life connects faith within everyday life at the same time as it fosters meaningful relationships. As congregations embody God's radical inclusivity, they become communities centered on God's love where diverse people open themselves to each other and the world.

Celebrating Diversity

Our worldview has been disrupted. We are now global citizens in a world where power is shifting and barriers are dissolving. As our global interdependence becomes evident, an ego-centric worldview is no longer acceptable. Whether experienced in the ethnically, religiously, socioeconomically, and politically diverse United States or in cross-cultural encounters around the world, loving our neighbor requires an ability to navigate difference and envision a world where all people thrive. As we saw in the last chapter, Globalization 3.0 calls out latent assumptions and challenges privilege. It demands we reexamine our preconceived ideas so we can honor and respect the distinctiveness of our neighbor. As we seek to see all people as God does—unique, unrepeatable subjects of God's love—celebrating diversity is necessary for living abundantly.

Christianity is always expressed within the particulars of culture, and so authentically loving others relies on our ability to relate within and across cultures. As we've discussed, *culture* "refers to the patterns of being, doing, and thinking that human communities share and to which they assign meaning."[29] Culture is a human construct and "is always a mixture of gift and fracture, truth and lies, nourishment and pollution, creation and sin."[30] Because we are socialized into it, our own culture is difficult to see. As our encounters with multiple cultures increase, loving others involves being aware of our particular cultural norms and enhancing our cultural intelligence, or ability to relate and communicate across cultures. In God's eyes, one culture is not privileged over another; cultures are simply different expressions of human community and meaning. Strengthening cultural intelligence expands our ability to love our neighbor and live abundantly in God's world.

Cultural intelligence is as much about us as others. Increasing our ability to relate across cultures enlarges our understanding of another's way of life and sheds light on ways culture is forming and shaping us. Because culture is multifaceted, cultural intelligence theory reflects on culture from four angles—knowledge, interpretation, perseverance, and behavior. These angles touch on our head, heart, actions, and drive.[31] Growing our capacity for loving neighbors across cultures is demanding, life-altering work. God knows that and invites us into it anyway.

Expanding our ability to reach across cultures nurtures an eco-centric worldview, contributes to the common good, and is critical to our call to love God and our neighbor.

God celebrates diversity, which is why God created each of us as unique, unrepeatable persons. Difference is not something to fear or avoid; it spices up life and adds flavor to the world. Difference, according to social scientist David Livermore, "can be racial, geographic, ethnic, economic, or ideological. When thinking of 'us' as compared to 'them,' the 'them' is what we mean by the Other. This term can sound pejorative, but it need not be as long as we keep in view that all of us are created in the image of God."[32] Our instinct is to turn away from difference, but God calls us to turn toward it. As we encounter others, both familiar and foreign, our understanding of God is stretched, and we see God's abundance more fully. Cultural intelligence is a perspective for seeing our neighbors as unique subjects of God's love and loving them in culturally respectful ways.

Our instinct is to turn away from difference, but God calls us to turn toward it.

Being connected while remaining distinct is the goal of all relationships. As our hearts are formed by God's compassion, we are able to open ourselves to the richness difference and diversity offer. Living in a world where many cultures coexist, Christians can practice open friendships in all aspects of their lives. Developing capacities for cultivating open friendships across cultures allows us to embrace difference and love authentically.[33]

Christians welcome the disruption of globalization because in God's economy, diversity and an eco-centric vision are celebrated. By deepening our awareness of how culture is embedded in our worldview, people of faith confess their own ego-centric understandings and open themselves to their neighbor as they seek authentic and respectful ways of loving others.

Contributing to the Common Good

The way we solve problems has been disrupted. Once, established institutions took the lead in addressing society's problems, but now digital platforms allow the masses to connect, create, share, and collaborate on their own. Today, nearly everyone has the means to broadcast their ideas and collaboratively solve problems. With few filters or regulations, almost anyone can use digital tools to voice concerns, create a community, and/or call for action. In a digital age, much of our collective action takes place "outside the framework of traditional institutions and organizations."[34] Power is shifting in favor of ordinary people. This shift creates the opportunity to reexamine our responsibility for contributing to the common good and to think about how we use our power.

Today's complex challenges must be addressed from multiple perspectives because they are multifaceted, are interconnected, and have long-term impacts. In an information age, people who curate information, interpret data, and generate knowledge add value. Since learning in the twenty-first century is best done connected to real-world challenges, tying external circumstances to personal concerns engages people in the learning process, makes it meaningful, and links it to lived experience. Cultivating communities of learning around today's challenges evokes people's personal power and provides avenues for contributing to the common good.

Since learning is an aspect of faith formation, this shift pushes congregations to move from an individual, content-focused approach toward a communal, real-world problem-solving approach. Such an approach taps into new power and builds on the collective action of learning communities. It also places learning within ministry, not as a separate activity. Harvard education professors Robert Kegan and Lisa Laskow Lahey believe deliberately developmental communities of learning are "incubators of capacity"[35] because they create capacity for addressing complex challenges and providing personal meaning by the way they organize themselves around their mission. Imagine the impact the church would make if it could ignite people's agency and release their capacity into the world.

Kegan and Laskow Lahey learned that personal aspirations, ongoing practices, and supportive communities are critical factors for creating deliberately developmental communities of learning. Aspirations provide the edge, focusing the learning and pulling the community into the future. Practices provide the groove, embedding the aspired future into daily activities. Community provides a home, establishing an environment of vulnerability and accountability.[36] Learning occurs when communal support and practices create the conditions for people to be stretched. Trust builds as people remain present with each other and stay the course, even as they disagree. As congregations become communities of presence and connect their ongoing practices to the world's complex challenges and people's aspirations, they join people in making meaning as they also contribute to the common good.

As Christianity unravels from society, the church needs new approaches to accompanying people in discovering a Christian way of life. Seeing a life of faith as a becoming journey and congregations as learning communities that contribute to good in the world offers the church a new posture for forming faith. Just as learning addresses real-world problems, so too does discovering a Christian way of life. As Christians come together to engage particular challenges of the world as respectful, authentic partners, they join God in co-creating the future God has promised. Embracing a twenty-first-century learning posture is key for forming faith today.

Abundant life is God's vision for the world. As we contribute to the common good in the world, we participate in God's unfolding kingdom. God's kingdom is experienced as much in mundane, ordinary life moments as in mountaintop experiences. The challenges of peace-making, eliminating poverty, and befriending the lonely are tackled in everyday encounters and personal relationships as well as grand initiatives and policies. When God's people see each person as a gift and embed practices such as listening and dwelling in the world into their daily encounters, they operate as if God's future is now. The Spirit is at work as much in the world as in the church. As people of faith anchor themselves in God's love and orient their actions toward

God's future, they discover how they can address the needs of the world. Despite being improvisational in many ways, congregations make meaning of contemporary circumstances as they cultivate communities of presence around God's table and invest in the common good.

People of faith contribute to the common good as they discover avenues for addressing real-life challenges and concerns. By embracing the communal dimension of learning, congregations become deliberate communities where people, personally and communally, discover their capacity for transforming the world. With an eco-centric view of abundant life, they lean into their countercultural role and participate in God's unfolding future as they love God and their neighbor.

Being One among Many

Christianity as an established religion has been disrupted. As the religious landscape in the United States becomes more fluid and Christianity relinquishes its societal privilege, discovering a Christian way of life includes learning to love our religiously diverse neighbors and witness to the risen Christ in an increasingly secular and religiously pluralistic era. While relational connections allow us to live graciously with one another, without a common vision and tools, it will be difficult to claim our Christian distinctiveness and find meaningful ways to collaborate across religious expressions.

What might an optimistic and expansive vision for abundant life among diverse religious expressions entail? Eboo

Patel, a Muslim born in India and raised in Chicago, has dedicated his life to imagining such a vision. His grandmother sparked his quest while he was visiting India. There, he saw her work with women fleeing domestic abuse and asked her why she did it. She said, "I do it because I am Muslim. This is what Muslims do."[37] That answer awakened his call for religions to profoundly engage the world.[38] The United States is a nation where diverse identities are respected, where relationships across cultures are encouraged, and "where promises are made to protect what is held in common."[39] Religion is an asset to this country and that vision. Diverse religions working together would exponentially enrich the well-being of all. The metaphor Patel uses is a potluck or communal feast where distinct communities are welcomed and contribute from their unique, distinct experience.[40]

What if we could agree that "no one thrives unless all thrive"? Such an agreement would prompt a vision that pushes beyond personal dreams, congregational visions, and faith traditions. It would be expansive enough to incorporate an eco-centric worldview and specific enough to need the particularities of each person, culture, and religion. It would require Christians to lean into the future in faith, confessing their belief in the risen Christ while also accepting the mystery of God. God created all things "to reflect God's life, beauty, and community."[41] God, as creator and redeemer, wants all of creation to live abundantly. Trusting in God's promises and oriented toward God's vision, can we, as Christians, open ourselves to an expansive vision of abundant life where all people contribute to the world's flourishing?

A vision for the world's flourishing does not begin with ideological debates or drafting theological statements. It begins in the particulars of relationships. Relationships are key to any vision of abundant life. Regular encounters that respect cultural and religious similarities and differences create the conditions for this expansive vision. Authentic relationships, framed with a spirit of mutuality and curiosity, guide the work. While it is impossible to walk in another's shoes, empathetic engagement and eagerness to learn from and with each other transform strangers into trusted companions and fellow sojourners. As we learn about the beliefs, practices, and ongoing challenges of others on the way, we find ways to create a just and trustworthy world together.

Inter-religious relationships are occasions for discovering our distinctiveness. Conversations with people of other religions (or no religion) force us to articulate our beliefs. Conscious of language, we tell our story of faith, become aware of assumptions, and share the role faith plays in our lives. Environments where people listen deeply and contribute freely make interfaith conversations rich experiences. God uses encounters of all kinds to strengthen and expand our faith. Studying sacred texts in community places our socialized beliefs and understandings into dialog with others. This is true of Christian communities as well as inter-religious ones. Because religious beliefs and

God uses encounters of all kinds to strengthen and expand our faith.

practices change over time, placing religious experiences within historical contexts also provides perspective. Inter-religious conversations challenge and hone our understanding of God and faith, and they also make working together toward a shared vision for abundant living possible.

The goal of this expansive vision is not conversion but tending the well-being of the whole world. Conversion is the work of the Holy Spirit. Christians witness to the gospel as they share God's transforming message and love their neighbor; the outcome of their witness is in God's hands. Because faith is a gift, our Christian witness contributes to the world's well-being as we love our neighbor.

Christians are invited to co-shape the future with God. Co-shaping a future where all of creation lives abundantly does not preclude people of other religions or no religion at all. As part one religion among many, Christians must recalibrate to an eco-centric vision of abundant living through the distinctiveness of the Christian faith. Claiming our God-given identity, testifying to the transformative power of God's grace, and respectfully loving our neighbor allow us to curiously engage other religions and work toward an expansive vision of abundant life.

Seeking Solidarity

On November 1, 2018, six days after the Tree of Life Synagogue shooting in Pittsburgh, I attended an interfaith service in St. Louis Park, Minnesota, a city that has cultivated a vision of living abundantly among its culturally and religiously diverse population, including a large Jewish population. The gathering was on All Saints Day. With Christian and Jewish friends in the community, I attended in solidarity.

I walked in as the service began. The sanctuary was full. The tone was somber. The mayor spoke and leaders from Christian, Jewish, and Buddhist faiths offered prayers and read sacred texts. The community joined in song. Candles were lit as each victim's name was read. Then a Jewish rabbi asked all the non-Jews to stand and invited those seated to look around. "These are allies," he said. "Lean on them today and in the future." Offering perspective from his own story, he noted, "This is a new day." I had goosebumps when he sat down. The interfaith prayer service embodied a future St. Louis Park had dreamed of for years. The social capital cultivated by so many in this city made this gathering authentic and meaningful. In the tragedy of death, life—and, specifically, abundant life—found a way.

The church is being disrupted and a new narrative is waiting to be written. The future is not fully here, but playgrounds of possibility offer glimpses of what is emerging. God's vision is for everyone to live abundantly. God's people have a role to play in making this happen. We are stewards of the future witness to God's ongoing presence in the world. Forming faith in the early decades of the twenty-first century is like navigating a wilderness terrain where everyone is an explorer, discerning is done on the way, and thriving requires the gifts and perspectives of all sojourners.

Do This and You Shall Live

In Luke 10, Jesus encounters a Jewish scribe (see Luke 10:25–37). The encounter begins with the scribe asking Jesus a question (Luke 10:25 NRSV): "What must I do to inherit eternal life?" Jesus responds by asking this expert in Jewish law what the law says. The scribe replies, "You shall love the Lord your God with all your heart, and with all your soul, and with all your strength, and with all your mind; and your neighbor as yourself" (Luke 10:27 NRSV).[42] Jesus then says, "Do this and you will live" (Luke 10:28 NRSV).

The significance of this encounter is best understood in context. First, the Jewish scribe saw himself as part of a community, so his initial *I* is also a *we*. "Confident of his own place in God's covenant community,"[43] his question is about who the *we* includes. Second, Jewish law already offered guidelines to the question "Who is my neighbor?"[44] so the question is either testing the law or Jesus. Third, the road from Jerusalem to Jericho was dangerous, and everyone knew it;[45] it was a vulnerable, isolated environment.[46] The hearers would not have been surprised that someone "fell into the hands of robbers, who stripped him, beat him, and went away, leaving him half dead" (Luke 10:30 NRSV). Fourth, Samaritans and Jews were enemies dating back to the eighth century BCE.[47] The scribe's operating assumption is that the scribe is not the Samaritan's neighbor. But what, exactly, does this story have to do with abundant life?

The scribe wanted to put conditions on God, and Jesus countered with an expansive vision. Jesus's view of abundant life had nothing to do lineage or following rules; compassion and showing mercy defined living abundantly. In this story it was the scribe's "enemy" who showed mercy to a nameless, faceless traveler. Coming upon a person beaten, robbed, and left for dead, the Samaritan was so filled with compassion he was compelled to act. Showing mercy is not a passive act removed from the messiness of life; showing mercy is love in action in God-forsaken places. In this life-or-death situation, a vulnerable person was met with overflowing grace and mercy. When Jesus says, "Do this, and you will live" (Luke 10:28 NRSV), he is putting forth an extraordinary challenge.

Thinking his neighbor was a member of his community or a vulnerable member of society, the scribe wanted to limit mercy. David Smith, the director of the Kuyers Institute for Christian Teaching and Learning, says, "Jesus's Samaritan story does not let us settle for showing kindness to our compatriots and keeping our cultural boundaries intact."[48] Jesus's response went beyond what the scribe could imagine, leaving him exposed and vulnerable. Showing mercy attends to the needs of others but it also changes our worldview. Being merciful flies in the face of an ego-centric view of life. In truth, all of us are vulnerable and in need of God's grace and the mercy of others.

A life of faith places us in wilderness territory. Traveling in the wilderness makes us vulnerable and highlights the need for showing mercy. We are the faceless, nameless traveler *and* the Samaritan. People formed by the cross rely on the mercy of a particular sojourner—Jesus. We can show mercy to others because Jesus first met us on the road. Reading this parable as the person in the ditch changes everything. Because "when we are needy enough, neighbor help from anybody at all is very welcome. It is from down in the ditch that we need to contemplate the question of who our neighbor is."[49]

God places agents of love on the road to encounter people in the ditch. Showing mercy puts God's love into action, not because someone deserves it or the law requires it, but because someone needs it. Every day there are occasions for showing mercy to our neighbor. Our neighbor may be known or a faceless stranger; the moment may be expected or a surprise. As we open ourselves to the world, we share what has already been given to us. As we put love into action, God's vision of abundant living breaks into the world, bringing God's unfolding kingdom near. Forces in the world will push back, but God's people are on the move, propelled by a power that creates out of nothing, brings life out of death, and discovers hope in despair. We are God's agents of love bearing witness to the transformational love of God.

People on the Move

#OptOutside began with an experiment for REI to boldly live their mission. By offering a challenge and providing a means for sharing stories, REI did more than that. As people scattered across the world participated, a one-time event grew into a movement. REI modeled the way and trusted their members and others to act. The collective response amplified each distinctive voice. Clear about the challenge, REI put forth a picture of a preferred future—and people joined. The future does not have to look like the past. Abundant life is possible for people journeying in the wilderness.

The church has a transformational mission to love God and our neighbor and an expansive vision for the well-being of all. We have the opportunity to reorient our lives and recalibrate our congregations toward God's promised future. All we have to do is engage people on the move. Christians need to integrate faith into their everyday life and live as if God's future is already among them. How can we share stories and encourage each other in this journey? How might the church help people live by God's economy with a different operating system? Disruptive forces have created openings for new patterns, stories, and operating systems. Learning from the future pushes aside old understandings and provides playgrounds of possibility. As the church learns to celebrate diversity, contribute to the common good, reclaim our relational existence, cultivate community, and become one religion among many, we will discover abundant life framed by God's grace and mercy. Is it time for some bold experiments?

Practice of Experimenting

What comes to mind when you hear the word *experiment*? An image from chemistry lab? Trying new recipes? Testing a new drug? No matter the environment, experimenting involves risk and the possibility of failure. Learning from the future and following Jesus both involve risk. But what kind of risk? Risk can be behavioral, such as firemen putting their safety on the line to save others; conditional, such as chemotherapy making a person vulnerable to getting sick; or probable, such as investing in markets or projecting the likelihood of something happening. Each is managed in a different way. The first is managed by decisions related to action, the second by controlling systems or environments, and the third by making judgments about the future. Seeing risk from different angles reminds us risk is already part of life, so dealing with risk requires learning when and how. Experimenting invites others into a shared experience of doing something new or different with the expectation of learning. Experimenting becomes a spiritual practice when we trust the Spirit with the risk of trying something new for the sake of God's promised future.

Experiments place underdeveloped ideas into concrete situations, anticipating critique, feedback, and input. Experiments can be prototypes, pilot projects, or exploratory programs. For years, I served in a congregation that encouraged experiments. Our experiments focused on communicating the gospel in various ways and were understood as a great way to learn from and with the congregation. Over time, experimenting taught us the value of taking risks and reframed our understanding of failure.

The high probability of failure makes experimentation feel risky, so seeing risk and failure as part of learning is crucial. I witnessed a great example of learning from failure in the men's quarterfinals of the 2018 Wimbledon tennis tournament. Four highly ranked players competed against four lesser-ranked players in highly competitive matching. Each match lasted several hours and went to four or five sets. Three top seeds made it through, but the number one seed lost to Kevin Anderson, the eighth seed. The number one seed was Roger Federer, one of the most decorated tennis players in history. In Roger's post-match interview he congratulated Kevin and credited his "big serve and his effective return"[50] for the win. He also shared how losing hurts, while at the same time motivating him to do better next time.[51] Roger Federer's drive to win is accompanied by his understanding that losing provides lessons winning never does. Used well, failure can exponentially advance our learning.

Our congregation had the opportunity to rethink failure when a speaker shared that the biggest difference between thriving and struggling is the ability to see failure as a learning opportunity. From that lesson, our leadership worked to create a culture that viewed failure as a learning moment. We named failure as "oh, fascinating" moments and talked through such experiences with colleagues to mine our learnings. As the phrase became a part of the culture, the shame around failure subsided. Taking risks and learning from failure require a supportive environment. As an iterative process, experimenting involves putting our ideas out in the world and learning from others' engagement with them. When trusted colleagues offer honest, critical feedback, a rich learning environment is created.

> Taking risks and learning from failure requires a supportive environment.

Playing is a common global activity; it is time or space set aside to image and explore (physically or mentally). Experimentation draws on play as it creates an environment where real-world demands are temporarily suspended and risk-taking is encouraged. With boundaries, an objective, and a few rules, play provides freedom to think differently, problem-solve, mimic others, collaborate, and release energy. As a fusion of creation and imitation, play places actions in context and transcends reality.[52] Play can be highly structured or free form; it can reinforce existing rules and subvert injustice at the same time. As the church navigates disruptions and learns from the future, play is a great vehicle for growing its capacity to experiment, learn from failure, and trust the movement of the Spirit.

For experiments to change the course of an organization, perseverance is necessary. Being clear about the goal is critical, especially when results fall short of expectations. Let's go back to our initial understanding of the word *experiment* and think about lab researchers. Such researchers amaze me with their discipline and perseverance; many dedicate their whole career to experimenting around one idea. Jim Allison is one example. Committed to fighting cancer, he used an unconventional approach to studying enzymes. Driven by the loss of many family members, he made "the first tenuous steps toward a generational breakthrough in the war against cancer."[53] But it took years before his work actually saved lives. All his days in the lab paid off in 2018 when Allison won a Nobel Prize.[54] His lifetime of work ultimately changed the direction of cancer research that now saves hundreds of lives, yet much of his life was learning from failed experiments and disappointing results.

Experiments matter most when engaging our most important work. Experiments that have staying power must be able to withstand failure, go through many iterations, and keep us engaged. Roger Federer and Jim Allison are examples of people who know this well. Along with their commitment and drive, they knew the power of learning from failure. Experimenting as a spiritual practice not only opens us to the Spirit; it also is a way to listen to and collaborate with our neighbors. Forming faith and witnessing to the gospel are endeavors worthy of our best energy, creative imagination, and experimenting.

Doing so can unleash unexpected results. Take the example of pastor and scholar Eugene Peterson, who loved Scripture. While serving a congregation, he experimented with communicating the Bible. His hope was to ignite a passion for Scripture within the people in that community. Twenty years later, his experiment turned into *The Message* Bible. *The Message* has now sold millions of copies and touched countless lives around the world.

Learning from the future involves risk and failure. Experimenting requires stepping out of our comfort zone. A supportive learning environment helps us take the necessary risks as we experiment with today's complex challenges. Forming faith in the twenty-first century is an endeavor worthy of bold experiments; playing it safe will not do. The world is in desperate need of holy experimentation so faith can come alive in the hearts and lives of each generation.

Practice of Particularity

What does abundant life look like, and how does loving God and our neighbor fit into our everyday life? The practice of vocation, or particularity, brings these concepts together. Take a moment and imagine living abundantly within the particulars of your world. Who is present? What is involved? Maybe living abundantly involves grandchildren or working in a chosen field. Maybe it imagines a medical breakthrough or food sustainability for people in your community. God's vision for abundant life comes through particulars.

Loving God and our neighbor is a simple command worthy of a lifetime commitment. A life shaped by this command weaves our story with God's story. It is within real relationships and specific circumstances that God extends love and we receive it. Missiologist Lesslie Newbigin says:

> The Bible invites us to see the real human life as a life of shared relationships in a world of living creatures and created things, a life of mutual personal responsibility for the created world, its animal and vegetable life and its resources of soil and water and air. This, and no other, is the real human life, which is the object of God's blessing and of his saving purpose.[55]

The practice of particularity helps us discover a Christian way of life through our stations in life. Our relationships, locations, and responsibilities are avenues for loving God and our neighbor and experiencing abundant life.

Kathleen Cahalan, a professor of pastoral theology and ministry, uses prepositions—the grammatical part of speech—to discover the particularities of call. She uses prepositions because they demonstrate that vocation is "relational, dynamic, and multiple."[56] They also "express the whole of our lives, even the places and experiences we never thought of as callings."[57] She sums up *calling* in this simple statement: "I am called *by* God, *to* follow, *as* I am, *from* grief, *for* service, *in* suffering, *through* others, *within* God."[58] These prepositions define how we can love the world with our own particularity.

God is the source of our callings. As unique, unrepeatable persons, our callings emerge from our God-given design. We discover our uniqueness across time in ordinary and transformational moments. While being aware of our gifts is important, the greater point is that God is the giver of those gifts. Given *by* God, we follow God into the world to love others as God loves us. Our callings give specificity *to* how we love God and our neighbor. That is both exciting and hard.

Try this exercise to illustrate the point: Think about your family and friends. What makes each of them unique? Now think about your co-workers, neighbors, and church acquaintances. What makes them unique? Reflect on the unique blend of gifts in your social circles. Now imagine God's vast network of people across the world. What would the world be like if everyone was using their gifts to their fullest potential? Each is called *by* God *to* follow God *into* the world.

Sometimes callings take us away *from* people, places, and/or situations *in* the midst of suffering. These callings can be redemptive, as they release pain and move us toward health. In this process, callings emerge from both pain and joy. For example, at the age of twenty-five, I faced the end of a marriage. During that painful time, I talked with people who had similar experiences. Those conversations demonstrated God's love and were tangible ways the church accompanied me during a rough period. In that season, my calling was to receive. Later, as I healed, I was able to accompany others.

Callings extend outward—for service in the world. Callings reorient us from ourselves to the world. As we embrace God's love for us, God turns us toward our neighbor. Our lives are not centered on personal fulfillment or happiness; meaning comes by contributing to a greater good. God intends to sustain and transform life—through us. We may only see a small part of the transformation, but God is surely changing the world through our service to the world.

Callings reorient us from ourselves to the world.

Our callings may come from different sources, but nearly always involve listening to and interacting with others. Through relationships and in community, God speaks and directs our lives. Both strangers and people we know may be avenues God uses to speak to us about how we might serve the world. Relationships are a petri dish for callings to be birthed and grown.

God not only dwells in the world; God also dwells within us. Paul says in 1 Corinthians 3:16 NIV, "Don't you know that you yourselves are God's temple and that God's Spirit dwells in your midst?" Sometimes, we sense God working in us, and sometimes, God seems silent. Either way, God is present. It is true for the young and curious as well as for the old and reflective.

We are always becoming the creatures God created us to be. Our wilderness journey can be a time of abundance, discovery, experimentation, and/or suffering—and we never know how it will present itself. A family friend discovered a new calling after a stroke. As he spent his final years in an assisted living facility, his spirit shone bright as his smiles and infectious love left its mark on the staff and residents. Ken knew God's calling throughout his life, but it never was as important as when he was confined to a wheelchair. God's Spirit is in us, allowing us to be a light in the world and a vehicle for loving others in the particularities of our lives.

We are God's beloved people, called to love the world. Each day, in each season, God's people love others through their relationships, roles, and responsibilities. How is God calling you today? Where has God been active in your story? How might God be pulling you into in the future?

Activities

1. *Do This and You Shall Live*—Read the Good Samaritan parable in Luke 10:25–37. Building on the ideas in this chapter, discuss the following questions:
    a. What do you think Jesus meant when he said, "Do this, and you shall live?"
    b. What insights did you gain learning about the context of this story? If you were to translate elements

of this story into our contemporary context, what would you do?

c. Why do you think Jesus left the traveler nameless and faceless?
d. Jesus ties being a neighbor to love in action. Using this definition, how have you been a neighbor lately?
e. God's vision of abundant life is different from the world's. What role does loving our neighbor have in God's vision?

2. *Articulate Abundant Living within Your Context*—Have each person call to mind someone who reflects God's love. Write down three or four reasons why that person reflects God's love. (For example: they are patient with others, love people who are different, work well through conflicts, make people feel important, listen.) Share the characteristics you named with the group. What themes emerged?

   Revelation 21 offers one picture of God's promised future. Thinking about your congregation, what is a picture of abundant living? In pairs, write down five to ten ideas. Then have pairs share with the group. After everyone has shared, highlight what stands out. If God were calling this group to co-shape abundant life in this community, what would you focus on? (If you are struggling, think about the REI story. Imagine a group of people sitting in a room somewhere trying to name the problem that pushed them to launch the #OptOutside campaign.)

3. *Participating in God's Mission*—Let's practice risking. Start with something silly. Create two identical obstacle courses with three or four stations that use different skill-sets. (For example: threading a needle, throwing a ball into a bucket, finding Waldo in a picture, and solving a math problem.) Divide into two teams and race through the course. Process what risk was like in this game.

   Brainstorm experiments for loving your neighbor. Generate as many ideas as you can, collecting them on a piece of newsprint. Give each person five stickers to choose the five ideas they like best. Then see which ideas have the most stickers. Write each of the five favorite ideas on a separate sheet of newsprint. Go through each idea asking, "What would experimenting with this idea entail?" Then vote on which experiment the group could do between now and your next meeting.

   At the next meeting, debrief the experiment. For example, if the idea was serving at the grocery store, share people's responses. If it was spending the afternoon at the neighboring care facility, what was it like engaging the people there? If it was helping elderly with yardwork, what was it like to enter someone else's property and serve in this way? After debriefing, talk about what it was like to risk doing something new or different in order to love your neighbor. Was the risk worth it? Why or why not? If the experiment did not go as planned, what did you learn? If you were to do a similar experiment, what would you do differently? What difference did this experiment make?

Now, think about areas of passion in your life and/or critical ministries of your congregation. What experiments could you do? What outcome would you hope for? What would need to happen to create a supportive learning environment? What feedback would be critical to learn from the experiment? After discussing some of these aspects, choose an experiment to carry out.

4. *Playgrounds of Possibility*—Based on the disruptive-forces activity in the previous chapter and the playgrounds of possibilities named in this chapter, what openings exist in your context to reimagine faith formation? How could those openings help your congregation accompany people in discovering a Christian way of life?

5

Travelers Gathering and Scattering: Sanctuaries, Campfires, and Outposts

> It is so much easier to venture far—not just in distance but also in terms of your willingness to experiment, take risks, and reach out to others—when you know that you're still tethered to a place called home, and to a real community.[1]

It was Sarah's idea—a girls BWCA canoe trip. She grew up canoeing with her dad and wanted her high school friends to have a similar experience. Her friends were city girls, so camping, canoeing, and "roughing it" would be new experiences. She enlisted our mutual friend Danette and me to turn her idea into a reality.

Danette and I gathered with the girls monthly for almost a year. During that time, we shared expectations, mapped a route, practiced setting up tents, and talked about what to wear. We learned how to paddle, portage, and steer a canoe. We prayed, laughed, and shared stories. The excitement grew with each gathering, and soon it was time to go.

On a sunny August morning, we headed north. The car was quiet for the first few hours, and then we saw Lake Superior. As the freeway transitioned to two-lane highway, the smells, sights, and sounds captured our attention, and our enthusiasm grew. We were no longer in the city; we were in the BWCA. Our preparation was over; we were here. We parked near our entry point and loaded the canoes. Leaving the comforts of home locked in the car, we pushed each canoe onto the lake. No one said anything for a few minutes. I'm still not sure who was more excited, the first-timers or veterans. In the quiet of the afternoon, you could feel the energy.

For three days we paddled pristine lakes, marveled at the scenery, and enjoyed a simple lifestyle. We cooked on a camp stove, took turns guiding the group, and shared camp duties. At the end of each day, we gathered around the campfire to tell stories, give thanks, and dream about the future. Without home and school pressures, we were present with each other and savored each moment. With wilderness wisdom and new perspectives, we had the best of both worlds. Soon, it was time to pack our tents for the last time and head home. After months of planning, in the blink of an eye, it was over.

We stopped for dinner in Grand Marais on the way back. We all needed showers but lingering in this liminal space provided one last chance to cherish each other's company and imprint our memories. As the sun set, we drove out of town with our favorite song playing, "This Road" by Jars of Clay: "All heavy-laden, acquainted with sorrow. May Christ in our marrow carry us home. From alabaster come blessings of laughter, a fragrance of passion, joy from the truth."[2] The song articulated our experience. These young women were acquainted with sorrow and the blessings of laughter. Our days canoeing were the capstone of this adventure, but the song spoke to our true adventure—a life of faith. It named what bonded us, spoke truth about our experience, and proclaimed our source of hope. Soon Sarah, Jill, Katie, and Darcy would be off to college, Danette and I busy raising our children, and this trip history. As we pulled into Sarah's driveway, I wondered if these ordinary days in the BWCA would make a difference.

Wilderness adventures bind people together. They form and change us. In the wilderness, relationships are deepened, priorities rearranged, and new perspectives gained. Sarah, with wisdom beyond her years, knew the formative power of wilderness experiences. What she did not realize was the impact this trip would have in cultivating an alternative way of life for all six of us.

Accompanying Our Becoming Journey

Central to recalibrating faith formation is claiming faith's role in our lives. Transformed by grace, faith reorients our life and places us on a lifelong journey of becoming. On this journey, our God-given identity, God's future, and our lived experience come together to form our unique personal story. As we love God and our neighbor through our roles, responsibilities, and relationships, we encounter God, make meaning, and taste abundant life. Because the present is informed by the past and future, our becoming is a "process, promise, and hope."[3] It is a process that identifies the dynamic, living character of faith in relationship with God and the world. It is a promise that claims God's faithfulness and commitment to humanity throughout history. It is hope that opens imagination and directs living toward God's promised future. Faith as a becoming journey widens the horizon of formation and accentuates it as a way of life.

Faith as a becoming journey widens the horizon of formation.

Being Christian is about loving God and our neighbor. This notion of faith sees God's activity as paramount and our actions as secondary; it decreases attention on what we do and increases attention on God. Discovering a Christian way of life starts with asking "What is God doing?" and then continues with discerning our actions in light of God's activity and the current circumstances. As faith forms, informs, and transforms us into co-creators of the future, we connect our story to God's story and join God in creatively and redemptively loving the world. Created for community and navigating the paradoxes of a world not yet as God intends, people of faith find allies, conversation partners, and guides. With God's view of abundant life as our lens for living, curiosity, compassion, and Spirit-led courage are just as vital as biblical knowledge, ethical living, and participation in church activities. Claiming, discerning, and joining God's activity, in our lives and in the world, are central to faith formation.

Faith formation is about accompanying people in this becoming journey as they discover a Christian way of life. Discovering a Christian way of life involves connecting our being, doing, and thinking with the beliefs, practices, and values of the Christian faith. As we live in solidarity with the world, two movements (gathering and scattering) and four dimensions of faith (gift, compass, witness, and agent) create a GPS-like operating system for orienting this way of life.

Cruciform Communities of Hope

Recalibrating faith formation also requires claiming the role congregations play. Congregations are communities formed by a cross. The life, death, and resurrection of Jesus Christ make congregations cruciform communities. The church, as the body of Christ, embodies a theology of the cross as it dwells in solidarity with the suffering and strives for the well-being of all. As congregations name evil, fight injustice, and enter God-forsaken places, God's promised future becomes visible. Believing life is more powerful than death, congregations look death in the eye and proclaim life's vigorous power. As signs, foretastes, instruments, and agents of God's love, local churches are drawn into the messiness of the world that is not yet as God intends. These cruciform communities, scattered and dispersed, extend God's love in the world.

The local church is a community where people are known and loved. Since faith is a relationship and Christianity is a relational way of life, love defines our lives and opens us to live in communion with others. Congregations gather in community to be formed and transformed into God's peculiar people. Aware of sin and our human desire to focus on ourselves, cruciform communities name brokenness, reconcile relationships, and practice forgiveness. With God hosting our gatherings, the church defends our relational nature as it becomes an open, inclusive community. Belonging and being loved are foundational for living full, abundant lives, so cultivating relationships shaped by God's creative and redemptive love is vital for cruciform communities.

Meaning-making is theological work that happens at the intersection of our understanding of God and our lived experience. Once people made meaning by applying institutional beliefs to their personal circumstances, but now meaning is made helter-skelter with loose religious connections, limited resources, and little time for reflection. With Christianity a lifelong journey, making meaning is less about crafting a coherent intellectual framework and more about navigating relationships and life circumstances. Congregations assist people in making meaning as they accompany them in discerning God's activity in light of current circumstances and a vision for abundant living.

Congregations do this as they put the particularities of people's lives in conversation with the peculiar nature of faith, allowing people to discover an "alternative tradition, gospel, and lifestyle."[4] Cruciform communities provide hope as they join people in the theological work of making meaning.

Cruciform communities dwell in their contexts. Congregations exist in particular locations with particular people. Their contextual realities define, bind, and guide them, while at the same time God's future directs and alters. God is always moving toward us, and cruciform communities follow God into expected and unexpected places. Dwelling in the world means not only being attentive to it, but also discovering how to respectfully and authentically be present within it. Learning to host and be hosted by neighbors strange and familiar is key for dwelling in God's world; God moves into the world as love flows through us. Reclaiming the contextual nature of forming faith as a cruciform community of hope is about getting real, being humble, and being messengers of hope within the realities of everyday life.

Leading from Below

To join God's activity in the world and people in their quest for making meaning in these disruptive times, our approach to forming faith needs to be recalibrated. Believing in God's transformational mission and expansive vision, it's time to trust God's scattered people to be agents of God's love in the particularities of their lives. Most approaches to forming faith are top-down, flowing from the church to people. In this model, the church is positioned as the expert and people as passive participants. With power held in structures and offices, change happens as the church (or a commissioned task force) researches, studies, and applies best practices. The main vehicles for change are strategic methods that work with organizational power and implement change through understanding. Change happens if and when the organization grafts new ideas into its current operating system. This strategic, top-down approach does not work for a church unraveling from society. Discovering how to form faith without cultural privilege, societal entitlement, and shared beliefs is critical for faith formation in the twenty-first century. Without external forces encouraging, fostering, or giving preference to Christianity, people of faith need a different approach for faith to become a way of life.

Practices of all kinds are a regular part of life. We have practices for parenting, learning, and taking care of our daily needs. Some practices are thoughtful; others are habits. Some embody our core values; others are circumstantial. Practices are influenced by an array of factors and do not rely on societal norms. Vincent Miller, a Roman Catholic theologian, sees practices as a way of disrupting the status quo and implementing change. Practices work at the behavioral level, can easily be repurposed, and incorporate ideas into simple, ordinary actions. If he wanted to change society's meaning-making "structures, rules, and power relations,"[5] he would take a practices approach. With practices, power flows up, making it a bottom-up approach that works with everyday people to change current realities. If a congregation wanted to push against networked individualism to reclaim people's relational existence, for example, it could repurpose behaviors reinforcing personalized, me-centered networking into behaviors that cultivate open friendships. This approach might start with a small-group face-to-face conversation about the highs and lows of people's weeks; follow up with people, checking in with each other via text each day; connect them again face-to-face the following week; and then share with the group their experience. Such an experiment could be tested for four weeks with people reflecting on their experience in the end. Does such an approach counter all of the other forces in someone's life? No, but it connects to everyday life, repurposing an existing practice toward another trajectory. Over time, and as more people participate, a practices approach to implementing change has the potential to transform people and communities, especially if we connect these practices with God's transformative power.

Let's contrast a practices approach with a strategic approach to transitioning from age-specific Sunday school to intergenerational faith formation. A strategic approach has the educational committee study intergenerational methods, share their findings, run a pilot, propose a change, and vote on the proposal. After a year of process, the new ministry goes forward or is rejected based on a vote. The markers of this approach are content, consensus, and voting. A practices approach invites a small group to participate in an intergenerational learning event, adds an intergenerational dinner to VBS, offers a summer family camp weekend, and pairs confirmation students with senior adults during

Lent. Each is an experiment that happens throughout the year in the midst of everything else. Feedback is gathered from each experiment, and ministry is modified, redirected, or replaced in an iterative process. This approach includes participants experiencing and reflecting on experiments as they move forward. Understanding emerges through practice over time, not before committing to new practices. The first approach has a clear process but is time-consuming, involves a small number of people, and culminates with consensus. The second approach is messy but involves participants immediately to shape the future and lets the process inform the outcome.

A practice-centered approach to forming faith is a GPS-like system that can automatically recalibrate as circumstances change. In this approach, practices provide the scaffolding for faith to form, inform, and transform our lives. In creating space for encounters with God and our neighbor, practices anchor faith, connect faith and everyday life, and have the potential to unify faith formation ministries across the church. Practices embed particular values and ways of being into daily living without prescribing programs or dictating outcomes. In other words, practicing our way into abundant living provides a way to discover a Christian way of life in a dynamic world. As congregations become cruciform communities, three types of practices employ this approach for accompanying people in discovering a Christian way of life: *sacramental,*

Practices embed particular values and ways of being into daily living.

incarnational, and *missional.* This section will describe each using the metaphors of sanctuary, campfire, and outpost.

Sanctuary—Cruciform Communities Are Sacramental

Christian communities have ancient practices to guide people in discovering meaning in relationship to God. These practices focus on God, anchor the local church, and transform human communities into the body of Christ. God's word and the sacraments form and transform us, providing the church dynamic stability across centuries. As a sign and foretaste of God's promised future, these practices allow congregations to discern their way in the midst of disruptions and uncertainty. Anchored and agile, cruciform communities provide travelers sanctuary, or holy space to gather with other travelers in God's presence. In other words, the local church has something to offer.

Sanctuary is often seen as synonymous with the local church's physical space, specifically their worship space. While worship space is a sanctuary, limiting sanctuary to church buildings restricts how cruciform communities fashion holy space and denies its portability. Sanctuary is more of an environment than a physical space. Practices related to Scripture, prayer, sacraments, or nature foster sanctuary environments. Communities are sanctuaries when people feel emotionally and relationally safe to be authentic and broken in God's presence. Sanctuary practices provide rest and renewal as time is reoriented, hearts are softened, and hope is restored. God's love is palatable in these environments, allowing travelers to let go of internal demands, name pain, and rest in the arms of God. Because God, not pastoral leadership or physical spaces, makes communities sacramental, sanctuary environments can be created anywhere two or three gather in God's name.

Throughout history, sanctuary has been created in various ways. As the Israelites wandered in the wilderness, the ark of the covenant held the Ten Commandments during their journey. Amidst a crowd at the Jordan River, God used John the Baptist and water to create sanctuary. Jesus created sanctuary around a table with bread and wine. The Bible is filled with stories of God creating holy spaces in different ways. Protestant Christians believe the ancient practices of baptism and holy communion create sanctuary as they anchor gatherings in God's creative and redemptive love. These practices link common elements (water, wine, and bread) to God's word, creating holy environments and renewing God's people. Gathering as the body of Christ and scattered in the world, God's people need sanctuary practices to encounter God.

Gathering around the word and sacraments in church buildings will likely continue in the twenty-first century, but limiting sacramental practices to Sunday mornings "at church" diminishes the role they can play in our life. Sacraments are core practices of the church where God is the primary actor. Tradition has made congregations, and in particular clergy-led worship, the exclusive community for these sacramental practices. If God is the host of the communion table, the transforming power in baptism, and the source of the word, perhaps we can also move sacramental practices outside congregational sanctuaries. An expanded view of the church's sacramental nature could release God's people to cultivate sanctuary environments using sacramental practices in their everyday lives.

We are sacramental people claimed by water and formed by a cross. In baptism, we die to the way of the world and are born into God's way of life. This transformation happens all at once and throughout our lifetime. Practices embed this transformation into our lives and remind us faith is a becoming journey. Perhaps making the sign of the cross on our foreheads and proclaiming, "I am a child of God, marked with the cross of Christ forever" at each worship gathering would help us remember this basic truth. Making the sign of the cross can also be done at home. Imagine roommates, family members, and senior adults thanking God and remembering their baptismal identity each time they gathered for a meal. If congregations can encourage and create meaning around making the sign of the cross in everyday life, this practice becomes a powerful tactic for forming an alternative way of seeing ourselves and the world. In the same way bread and wine anchor congregational gatherings, they could also anchor gatherings of family and friends. Through bread and wine, God forgives and unites diverse people. As people whose nature is to focus inward, communion litanies could assist us, dispersed in the world, to reorient our lives around God's grace and mercy. People of faith need spaces to encounter God, remember God's promises, and be united as unique and diverse people. Remembering our baptism and the night Jesus was betrayed could be formative practices exercised not only in our congregational gatherings, but also in smaller gatherings around the ordinary, mundane aspects of our lives.

This book has introduced several sanctuary practices. *Dwelling in the word* is a practice that draws our attention to God through God's word. Dwelling in Scripture is a sanctuary practice where God's word is heard in light of people's current circumstances and through their neighbor. *Reflecting on experience* is a practice for gaining perspective and making meaning. Wrestling with God's presence in the world not yet as God intends enhances our ability to live abundantly. As we explore our God-given identity, we have the opportunity to internalize our call and realign our lives around God's mission. *Sabbath* is a practice rooted in our need for rest. Living in a 24/7 society has increased the need for personal Sabbath. Sabbath practices provide rest for our bodies, space for attending relationships, and time for tending our soul. As we participate in sanctuary practices, within church gatherings and scattered in the world, God's love becomes a rudder for our lives and renews us for loving our neighbor.

Campfire—Cruciform Communities Are Incarnational

With this in mind, the local church has relationships to tend. Relationships, not content, are the primary means for discovering a Christian way of life. Yet for decades, faith formation has focused primarily on knowledge. Beliefs are part of forming faith, but the essence of faith is love. A life of faith centers on loving God and neighbor; it is a relational endeavor. Knowledge about

God, the church, and a Christian way of life must be set within relationships formed, informed, and transformed by God's love, leading to faith formation. The church is an instrument of God's love as it embodies God's grace and mercy. Centered and open, cruciform communities are like campfires, communities of presence for travelers to be with and for each other.

Anyone can create campfire gatherings. The instructions are simple: Build a fire (literally or figuratively), invite people, and be present. A campfire's basic form makes it easily replicated. Its warmth draws people in, and relational connections keep people engaged. Telling stories and pondering life provide the agenda. Leadership is shared and intimacy created as participants voice their joys and struggles. Campfires are powerful, informal gatherings that cultivate communities of presence and incarnate God's love.

Everyone needs communities where they are known and free to be themselves. In today's accelerated world, this need is even more urgent. Filled with ordinary, mundane aspects of life, campfire communities are messy, real, and authentic. In these informal communities, no one is the expert and dilemmas do not need to be solved. Participants come and go, and people participate at the level they choose. As people are each seen as a unique, unrepeatable gift, campfires become sacred communities where intimate relationships are cultivated. Campfire practices provide environments for encountering others and creating connections across difference. As participants are valued and relationships made, people are awakened to the simplicity and expansiveness of their relational identity. With storytelling and listening the primary vehicles, campfire-like settings allow people to open themselves to others and the Holy Spirit as they reflect on their lived experience. If sanctuaries are holy spaces, campfires are communities where people feel emotionally and relationally safe and where difference is welcomed.

Convening gatherings is not enough for cultivating meaningful community. Congregations become relationally meaningful as they nurture belonging and practice open friendships. As one of the few communities in society nurturing bonding and bridging relationships, congregations can intentionally convene diverse groups of people and host conversations on important topics. People can come together based on geography, life stage, passions, or experience. Congregations could design communities of presence around generational intersections, affinities, or life transitions. Congregations can host public forums, collaborate with unique partners, or become neighborhood hubs. If the local church modeled and empowered bonding and bridging relationships, it would create a strong relational foundation for forming faith. As twenty-first-century travelers navigate economic, social, cultural, ethnic, and religious diversity, campfire practices are increasingly important.

There are several campfire practices already suggested in this book. *Telling faith stories* is a practice many congregations have lost. Storytelling places meaning-making in the midst of everyday experiences and allows God's activity to be seen through someone's lived experience. This practice is essential for witnessing to faith in a religiously pluralistic world. *Listening* is a practice rooted in valuing others that can be easily integrated into daily life. Listening requires setting aside our self-centered nature and being emotionally present with another; growing our capacity to listen increases our ability to encounter difference. *Cultivating Christian communities* is a practice centered on our relational identity, honoring our uniqueness, and making our lives dependent on others. Open friendships embody God's love as people explore unique relationships with others. Seeing everyone as valued persons is an alternative way of being in the world. Campfire practices aid congregations and God's faithful people scattered in the world to open themselves to others and be vessels of God's incarnate presence.

Outposts—Cruciform Communities Are Missional

Maybe the local church has something to do. After all, the world needs agents of love; God's promised future relies on God's people loving the world as God does. Christians join God in loving the world as they heal, tend, and reconcile through the particulars of their lives. God's kingdom unfolds and we co-create the future within and through our relationships with family, friends, and co-workers, as well as strangers, enemies, and adversaries. Seeing all places as having the potential for life, people of faith embrace God's vision of abundant living as they engage their contexts and contribute to the common good. Grounded in

God's promised future relies on God's people loving the world.

sacramental communities and nurtured by incarnational communities, travelers also need outposts, or missional communities where they can live in solidarity with their neighbors dispersed in the world.

Outpost stations are often scattered in wilderness areas. They serve as gathering points for travelers to seek shelter, exchange information, and get resources. Outposts expect strangers, provide basic supplies, and specialize in navigating their surrounding terrain. Outposts exist within a greater network, in which additional resources and expertise are shared as needed. Outposts come in different forms; some have guides and plan routes, others rent equipment and provide overnight shelter, and others are primitive shelters without personnel. Outposts are wilderness hubs that empower travelers to navigate dynamic contextual conditions and provide important resources for the common good.

As God's people dwell in the world, outposts are critical. Outposts accelerate problem-solving and resource-sharing. Discerning where and how God is moving, experimenting with abundant living, and collaborating for the common good, outpost communities rely on diverse relational connections and the ability to see beyond present circumstances. As communities of learning, outposts support travelers and foster their entrepreneurial spirit. As agents of God's love, God's people need conversation partners as they wrestle with loving their neighbors amidst contextual complexities. With sacramental communities centered on God and incarnational communities focused on relationships, missional communities engage the world.

Missional communities identify assets that can be used for the common good. They draw attention to particular real-world challenges and set the table for diverse partners to collaborate or create experiences for encountering and reflecting upon difference. As they do, they not only accompany people in discovering a Christian way of life, but they also equip them to discern their own calling and share God's love in the world. Missional practices recognize that faith is lived in the world where God is already active.

Throughout this book, several outpost practices are named. *Dwelling in the world* is a practice that turns our attention outward. Hearing stories and looking for God's presence in the world are exercises in humility and curiosity. Letting go of assumptions and opening our hearts to others expand our vision of what is possible. *Being hosted* is a practice that lifts up the posture of humility. It calls for vulnerability, trust, and curiosity by entering others' spaces. As we are hosted, we reimagine faithful living through our interactions with diverse peoples and cultures. *Particularity* is a practice that recognizes God in the specifics of life. It is where our unique God-given design intersects with our roles and responsibilities, and the contexts where we live. Particularity provides concrete circumstances for loving God and our neighbor. *Experimenting* is a playful practice at the intersection of risking the known and trusting the Holy Spirit. It orients our attention to the future, sees failure as an opportunity for learning, and is best done in community. It is named here as an outpost practice, but in reality, it cuts across all three practices; nudged by the Holy Spirit, experimenting is where holy disruption meets playgrounds of possibility. Outpost practices accompany travelers in discovering their capacities and empowering them to join God in co-creating the future, personally and communally.

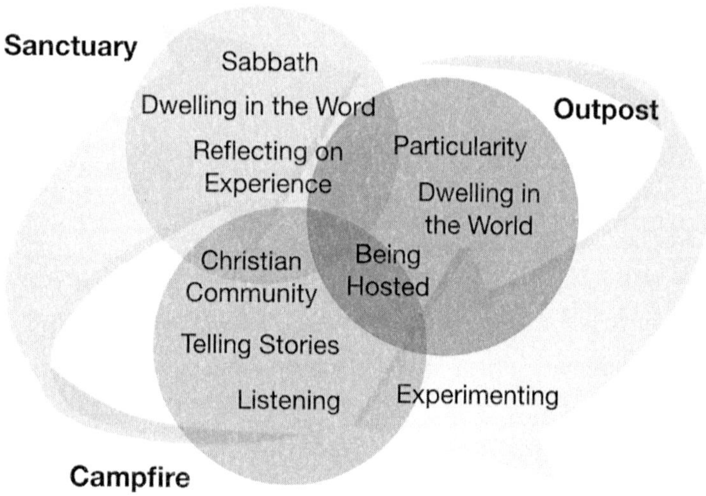

A Practice-Centered Approach to Forming Faith

Congregations become cruciform communities of hope as they engage in sacramental, incarnational, and missional practices. Distinctive and overlapping, these sets of practices encourage faith to happen in everyday experiences. Centered on our call to love God and our neighbor, a contextual approach to faith formation sees the world as the location for living faith, and practices as the best way for the local church to accompany travelers on their lifelong journey of faith.

Igniting a Movement

Maybe it's time for a movement. Today's disruptions and complexities have created the conditions for something transformational to happen. Movements start small, with one person willing to risk (and look foolish) before another joins in. As two become a small group, momentum starts. As their actions touch on a need or opportunity, the group gains traction and becomes a movement.[6] In a similar way, a practice-centered approach to change entices ordinary people to assimilate practices into their everyday life. What begins as one or two actions evolves into a way of life, and God's people practice their way into the future.

People of faith are longing for faith to help them make meaning of their lives. Some can articulate their longings, and others cannot. What we do know is the old approaches were not designed for our current context. In these disruptive and uncertain times, forming faith requires returning to the basics, setting our eyes on the future, and risking for the sake of the gospel. As the local church engages its particular contextual challenges, we practice our way into the future by working with diverse partners. An eco-centric vision for the well-being of all will open us to new relationships and practices. It is time to step forward in faith and ignite a movement reimagining faith formation.

It is hard to plan a movement, but sometimes it just happens, as was the case with a group of pastors in Denver. They gathered to think, dream, and pray about how they might serve the community. When they asked the mayor how they could help, he said, "The majority of issues that our community is facing would be eliminated or drastically reduced if we could just figure out a way to become a community of great neighbors."[7] Relationships are more effective than programs, he said, because they are "organic and ongoing."[8] That reply sparked an idea. How might local churches work together to cultivate a community with great neighbors? Their work began with church leaders doing a sermon series and offering resources, but preaching about and getting to know your neighbors are two different things, so the pastors reoriented their time and energy to get to know their neighbors.[9] Humbled by the mayor's reminder of God's command, they turned their focus to loving God and their neighbor and sparked a movement.

Maybe loving God and our neighbor is all we need for living abundantly. Reflecting on what helped them in Colorado, Pastors Jay Pathak and Dave Runyon said,

> When Jesus was asked to reduce everything important into one command, he gave us a simple and powerful plan that, if acted on, would literally change the world. This simple plan also offers us a different kind of life. It's a way of living that makes sense and brings peace to people's souls. Whenever we center our lives around the Great Commandment and take very literally the idea and practice of loving our neighbor, there's great freedom, peace, and depth of relationship that come to our lives. By becoming good neighbors, we become who we're supposed to be. As a result, our communities become the places that God intended them to be.[10]

As local churches accompanied people into loving their neighbor, they challenged them to dwell in their literal neighborhood. People mapped their neighborhood and wrote down who lived in the eight houses around them. They added any details they knew about their neighbors and how often they communicated.[11] What they discovered was that only 10 percent knew the names of all eight neighbors, 3 percent knew information about each person, and less than 1 percent had any ongoing relationship with all eight neighbors.[12] The brutal truth is we cannot love our neighbors if we do not know them. Loving God and our neighbor is not a generic command; it only works when our neighbors have particular names and locations. We have real neighbors whom God wants us to love. It is time we get to know them.

> We cannot love our neighbors if we do not know them.

What started as twenty local churches now includes over 70,000 people and over 1,000 congregations.[13] Pathak and Runyon said,

> It's difficult to quantify the results of good neighboring. What we do know is that when people get to know their neighbors, good things start happening. Real relationships are formed. And these relationships make a difference. Neighbors start to work together. They shovel driveways, get to know aging neighbors, notice strangers walking around, and help each other in a pinch. These small acts add up to something significant.[14]

As we tether our lives to God's love and weave faith into our everyday experiences, the world is changed from the bottom up.

The art of neighboring is just one example of how the local church can ignite a movement. Anything that embeds abundant living into the particularities of our context has the potential, but it has to involve practices and be concrete. As the church engages the playgrounds of possibility created by today's disruptive forces, it has the ability to change lives and create a new narrative for the church. Addressing the longings and concerns which lie below the surface, congregations cultivate meaningful relationships and practice their way into the future. They act as communities of learning prepared to accompany people in discovering a Christian way of life.

Guided by the Spirit

Imagine what it was like discovering a Christian way of life in the first century. For fifty days, the apostles waited for the Spirit. When she boldly came, she disrupted their lives, along with many of the travelers gathered in Jerusalem. Three thousand people were baptized in the first gathering of the apostles. Jesus called the disciples to witness not only to Jerusalem, but also to Judea, Samaria, and the ends of the earth (Acts 1:8). And so, the scattering began. Believers spread out from Jerusalem and began planting communities of faith in various locations along the trading routes of Palestine. With no patterns to follow or church planting books to read, the apostles went forth, guided by the Spirit.

As the first witnesses, the apostles discerned the trail on the way, orienting their lives to God's transformational love and promised future. The church, made up of a loose network of Jesus followers, accompanied each other as they discovered a Christian way of life. They relied on shared practices, social networks, and the Spirit. As Jewish and gentile converts from particular locations came together to form one body, there were growing pains. Forming faith in the midst of these diversities was complex. What made it possible was their unwavering commitment to God's mission and their willingness to adapt.

An early debate surfaced regarding how Jewish practices should impact Christianity's new expression. Knowing that the Jews had been God's chosen people and that gentiles were now part of the future made the debate messy. In Acts 15, this concern is addressed at a council debating the practice of circumcision. Circumcision was a Jewish practice signaling their faithfulness to God. Paul believed God's grace was sufficient and spoke in favor of gentile believers not needing to participate in this practice. He said,

> God, who knows the human heart, testified to them by giving them the Holy Spirit, just as he did to us; and in cleansing their hearts by faith he has made no distinction between them and us. Now therefore why are you putting God to the test by placing on the neck of the disciples a yoke that neither our ancestors nor we have been able to bear? On the contrary, we believe that we

> will be saved through the grace of the Lord Jesus, just as they will. (Acts 15:8–11 NRSV)

The council had a decision to make. At this important crossroads, the church erred on the side of grace. When in doubt, trust the Holy Spirit.

The early church was a people on the move. After the council's decision, Paul was back on the road planting churches to the ends of the earth. He headed north into new territories with Silas and Timothy. Yet their way was blocked as they were "kept by the Holy Spirit from preaching the word" (Acts 16:6 NIV). So they readjusted their route and found "the Spirit of Jesus would not allow them to" go that way either (Acts 16:7 NIV). Rerouting one more time, they stayed the night in Troas, where Paul received a vision telling him to go to Macedonia (Acts 16:9–10 NIV). To us as twenty-first-century travelers, this situation sounds frustrating, yet Paul, Silas, and Timothy do not seem to be deterred. Their operating system allowed them to trust God and rely on the Spirit. In fact, they believed recalibrating was a direct result of God. For Christ followers, this is a valuable lesson—clarity on our call lets us see God's presence even in recalibrations.

Once in Philippi, a city in Macedonia, Paul and crew lay low for a few days (an interesting response after all their work to get there). On the Sabbath, they went to a place of prayer and encountered a group of women. Open to their teaching, the women listened to them and one of them, Lydia, asked to be baptized. Then she invited them to be hosted at her home. They followed, listening to the Holy Spirit and relying on the hospitality of strangers.

Three lessons from these events stand out for forming faith. First, *our current time is not the only complex era for forming faith.* Navigating uncertainties and discerning the trail in the first century is hard to imagine, yet because of people like Paul, Silas, Timothy, and Lydia, you and I have faith. Millions of people between the first century and today have participated in God's mission and shared the good news of the gospel. Faith is a wilderness journey in all eras, and we are indebted to previous generations' witness and faithfulness. I am especially thankful for my grandparents and great-grandparents who, as immigrants to the United States, discovered a Christian way of life while navigating a new culture and assimilating in a new land. Their everyday lives stewarded the future witness of faith in the midst of the particularities of their time and location.

Second, *the mission is God's, not ours.* I cannot imagine how hard it was for Jewish leaders in the early church to set aside their assumptions and operating system of faith. Trusting in the Spirit, they shifted from seeing only themselves as God's chosen people to including gentiles in God's vision. They opened themselves to God and others, learned to cross boundaries, and embraced diverse expressions. When the way forward was unclear, they focused on the one leading—God. Remembering that the mission is God's and trusting the Spirit when in doubt are critical for forming faith today.

Finally, *discovering a Christian way of life is relational.* It is not individualistic. The early church relied on council leaders, apostles, and local leaders working together. Each had different roles, responsibilities, and gifts. God's church is a dynamic, multidimensional body. Our gifts, experiences, backgrounds, and relationships are all needed in this expansive mission. Gathered and scattered, we use our varied gifts and vocations to serve differently. Some will serve primarily through sacramental practices, others through incarnational practices, and yet others through missional practices. When we are at our best, all work toward abundant living for all people. With sanctuaries, campfires, and outposts dispersed throughout the world, wilderness travelers will discover a Christian way of life that is accompanied by God's church.

You Never Know

Today, Danette and I are empty-nesters, and Sarah and the other girls have careers and families. Katie has traveled the world teaching and exploring different cultures. Her smile lights up a room. Darcy is married and has a sweet little girl. She works in the medical field and uses her gifts to serve people at home and far away. Jill is a teacher and event organizer who employs her creative gifts to create amazing experiences for young people and adults. She loves being an aunt and spending time with her husband and dog. Sarah is a mother of three living in her husband's home state of Virginia. She and her husband have navigated graduate school and work while raising their family.

We do not see each other very often, but we do keep in touch. Years have passed, but the memories of our canoe adventure still have a special place in our hearts. Faith united us then and unites us now. We knew we were subjects of God's love designed to live in relationship. This foundation allowed us to be our flawed and beautiful selves. With our eyes set on God's vision of abundant living, we created space for pushing against the claims the world wanted to place on us and allowed the Spirit to form, inform, and transform our lives. Able to live in the midst of paradox, we trusted God's presence even when the world was not yet as God intended. Somehow, monthly gatherings and three days canoeing generated within us the capacity to discover a Christian way of life as we navigated uncertainties.

Just like I cannot fully explain what happened that summer, I also cannot fully articulate how exploring 1,238 miles on my bike changed me. In those months of navigating new terrain, I discovered a new way of being in the world. "Explorer mode" got me to slow down and loosen my grip on efficiency as it also allowed me to see failure's role in learning and awakened me to my surroundings. Explorer mode was not as scary as I thought. The adventure left me with awe and gratitude, a feeling of being connected to a greater whole, and the ability to see how the present can gift the future.

As I listen to church leaders share their experiences of leading God's church, I am grateful for their work and in awe of what God is up to. The church is not dead; it is recalibrating as God's people return

> The church is not dead; it is recalibrating as God's people return to the basics and engage their neighbors.

to the basics and engage their neighbors. Joining God's creative and redemptive mission of loving the world within our contexts and particularities is an abundant way of life. May God bless us in this journey as God's love overflows into the world.

Practice of Sabbath

As I write this, it is a snow day in Minneapolis. It is February 20, and today's seven inches made this the snowiest February on record. On our fifth snow day this season, Minnesotans are being forced to let go of control. After recalibrating our day, we loosen our ties to external demands, reorient our mindset, and enjoy being home. In other words, snow days are unplanned Sabbaths.

The first chapter of Genesis describes God separating light from darkness, partitioning sea from land, placing stars in the sky, and scattering animals across continents. God's creativity and handiwork are evident, but Genesis also notes God rested. In fact, "God blessed the seventh day and made it holy, because on it he rested from all the work of creating that he had done" (Gen 2:3 NIV). As people created in God's image, we join God in co-creating and resting.

My natural inclination is to keep going, and resting is hard. But a few years ago, that changed. I connected with Hayim Herring, a Jewish rabbi, for a work project. As we began, Hayim shared his Sabbath-keeping practice. From sundown on Friday to sundown on Saturday, he was not accessible. As a Christian, I was curious about his practice and wondered how he did it in today's world. He explained that his practice included a Shabbat meal, attending synagogue, spending time in prayer, reading the Torah, and abstaining from many "worldly" luxuries, including automobiles and technology. During the project, my curiosity turned to admiration as I discovered the discipline and joy this sacred practice held for him and his wife. At the end of our project, my husband and I were invited to share a Shabbat meal with them. It was a sacred evening with great food, wonderful hospitality, Hebrew prayers, and unforgettable fellowship. Working alongside Hayim made me rethink my Sabbath-keeping practice.

Sabbath is a time for rest or ceasing from work. The Ten Commandments make Sabbath part of life's rhythm. Exodus highlights how Sabbath is built into the order of the creation, and Deuteronomy focuses on demonstrating "our obedience to the One who created us and redeems us."[15] God's creative and redemptive love is part of Sabbath keeping. We remember how God created us and observe what God desires for our life. Christian Sabbath is not as regulated as Jewish Sabbath, but it is a discipline. Guidelines make Sabbath keeping a thoughtful and intentional practice. Theologian and professor Rob Muthiah, in *The Sabbath Experiment*, offers seven guidelines for Sabbath keeping: prepare, begin with a meal, embrace rest, worship in a local church, opt out of buying and selling, put aside mediated devices, and end with a meal.[16] Guidelines provide the skeleton for the practice, but cannot cultivate its spirit. Sabbath is a gift to humankind, a day to remember God and our relationships, a time to slow down in a fast-paced world, and the chance to be in God's creation. It is part of how we were designed, and it is a gift from God. Remember, it is "God who in Sabbath rest receives our worship and offers us the most abundant life possible, a life rooted in God's creation, a life redeemed and transformed by the saving work of Christ, and a life filled with the Spirit who leads us forward into God's preferred future. It is a future we taste each week when we enter Sabbath time."[17]

Christians can learn from our Jewish brothers and sisters about the countercultural nature of Sabbath keeping. At our Shabbat meal, I asked Hayim's wife what this practice was like for her as a lawyer. She responded, "When we lived in New York, it was easier. Everyone at my firm was Jewish. But when we moved to Minnesota, I knew it would be harder. When I took this position, I told my colleagues and clients that you have me 24/6, but from Friday evening to Saturday evening, I'm not working." Her witness inspired me.

A few years ago, I invited students in a leadership course to engage in a Sabbath experiment. For four weeks, they practiced weekly Sabbath keeping using the guidelines offered above. At the end of the course, I was surprised at their responses as they reflected on the experience. Almost everyone thanked me and shared how meaningful it was, but few felt they could continue it after the course. They did it as an assignment, but without incentive, it was too hard to continue.

We are created to work and rest. Tending both is part of living abundantly. What do you need to cease from doing? Sabbath keeping is a spiritual practice that celebrates life and reconciles us to God and each other. As we engage in Sabbath practices, we steward our lives and witness to God's alternative way of living. Experiment with Sabbath and find one or two others to join you.

Practice of Cultivating Christian Community

Faith is relational and cultivating Christian community is critical for forming faith. That truth cannot be overemphasized. Youth ministers know what many congregations take for granted—all ministry rests on a relational foundation of Christian community. Christian community translates the beliefs of faith into action. When such a community is cultivated, real-world concerns surface; questions about God, sin, and meaning are expressed; and God's presence is recognized. Christian community is the holding environment for forming faith, and cultivating such a community does not happen accidentally.

Forming Christian community is a practice that can be learned. Four elements are core to this practice: *engagement, embodiment, community care,* and *being open*. The first is engagement. Living in a hyperconnected, digital age is weakening relational connections and diminishing authentic engagement. Cultivating authentic engagement strengthens relational ties and transforms congregations from loosely connected relationships to caring communities. As congregations connect people to God and each other, they create the conditions for intimate relationships and meaningful community. As congregations carefully tend connections, all people are valued, good questions are asked, curiosity is encouraged, and the emotional state of people is noticed. All of these factors contribute to the overall health of the community. Engagement is a basic element of Christian community. Probing beyond the pleasantries and getting to know the persons gathered have exponential value in cultivating community.

The local church is an incarnational community that embodies (the second element) Christian beliefs and witness. Being thoughtful about living our theological commitments is part of what makes Christian communities unique. Christians are peculiar people who practice forgiveness and reconciliation. How is forgiveness embodied in your congregation? Congregations stand up for injustice and see all people as created in God's image. What tactics could your community of faith employ to embody equality? Christian communities are spaces where people wrestle with meaning and find hope. What spaces does your congregation have for people to make meaning and find hope?

We are broken people with visible wounds and hidden scars. Illness and abuse are among us. Congregations cultivate Christian community as they recognize these realities and become communities of care (the third element). Care takes many forms, from holding each other in prayer to listening to bearing each other's burdens and walking with people in hard times.[18] Over the years, congregations have often narrowed caregiving to pastors, seeing them as professional caregivers. This has increased pressure on pastors and let the rest of the community off the hook. Pastors do have responsibilities in caring for people, but so does everyone else. Caring is both a specialized ministry and a practice everyone is called to participate in. Being part of a community means caring for others in the community.

Christian communities are open (the last element) to people not yet connected. Christian communities exist because God's love unites them and draws people in. They are not clubs. Love is foundational, and love reorients us, personally and communally, toward the world. This open spirit is the posture the local church has for people not yet among them. God's openness means there is always room for another person and their story. A Christian community never reaches full capacity.

Professors Angela Reed, Richard Osmer, and Marcus Smucker call the ministry of cultivating Christian community spiritual companioning: "Spiritual companioning is a way of accompanying others in intentional relationships of prayerful reflection and conversation that help them notice God's presence and calling in their lives, local communities, and the world. It involves the provision of support and accountability in responding to God's invitations."[19] It is mutual accompaniment, where participants give and receive, learn and teach, support and rely on others. Caring and accompanying each other come from an external source—God. As we reimagine the expression of church fitting for today's environment, "the ministry of spiritual companioning is an important element in the life of a congregation to help us learn how to keep opening up to God and to one another."[20] Faith is relational, and cultivating Christian community is critical for forming faith.

God's openness means there is always room for another person and their story.

Activities

1. *Guided by the Spirit*—Read Acts 16:1–16. Working with the insights in this chapter, discuss each theme using the questions provided.

   Theme 1: *Our time is not the only complex era for forming faith*. Thinking about the first century and your own ministry context, what similarities and differences do you see? What can we learn about forming faith from first-century Christians navigating cultural and religious differences? What united the first-century church and guided their daily living?

   Theme 2: *The mission is God's, not ours.* Is it a relief or scary to know the mission is God's? Why? What does grounding faith formation in God's activity mean to you? When have you sensed the Spirit guiding you to witness to God's story or be an agent of God's love? When have you sensed the Spirit guiding you to risk?

   Theme 3: *Discovering a Christian way of life is relational (all of God's people are needed).* How can you contribute to your congregation finding its way? Who have been unexpected partners for forming faith in your context? What changes could your congregation make to expand their leadership capacity?
2. *Practice Sabbath*—Sabbath keeping can be done on various levels. An introductory level could be picking one aspect of life that distracts you from loving God and your neighbor and abstaining from it one day a week for six weeks. On

those days, pay attention to how you feel and what is different. A deeper level could be setting aside a certain amount of time each week to cease from working. During this time, experiment with different Sabbath practices. Maybe you focus solely on relationships, serving others, or simply tending to your soul. Journal about your experience and look back at the end of the six weeks to see what you discovered. An "all-in" level could be engaging in Muthiah's Sabbath experiment of a weekly 24-hour household Sabbath. Decide how many weeks to experiment with Sabbath keeping and give yourself grace if something interrupts and requires your attention. If you can, find another family or household to engage in Sabbath keeping with you. Talk about your experience at the end.

3. *Contextual Approach to Faith Formation*—Faith is a lifelong journey of becoming. Loved unconditionally, people of faith respond by loving God and their neighbor. Gathered in Christian community and scattered into the world, God's people discover a Christian way of life as they discern and join God's activity in their lives and the world. Accompanying people in this journey is how the church forms faith. What could that mean for your congregation? This five-step process weaves together activities from each chapter to help you custom-design faith formation for your ministry setting.

   First, review your understanding of faith formation developed in chapter 2. What would you change or add in light of what you have learned in this chapter? Review your understanding of faith formation based on your discussion and revise it as needed.

Second, review how consumerism, the Digital Revolution, the Information Age, globalization, and religious pluralism are impacting your context (see the activity in chapter 3). What are the top two or three challenges you face related to forming faith?

Third, review the experiments you tried in chapter 4. What did you learn? What experiments might connect your understanding of faith formation and your top two or three contextual challenges? Name some possible experiments.

Fourth, reflect on how your congregation accompanies people as they seek to discover a Christian way of life while scattered in the world. Using the three sets of practices named in this chapter, list ways your congregation engages sanctuary, campfire, and outpost practices. What practices do you want to enhance? What new practices might your congregation incorporate? What practices might your congregation drop given your current understanding of faith formation? Discern one or two action steps to move forward.

Finally, read through what you named in each step and reflect on what you see. (If you have time, review the faith formation audit from chapter 1.) Give members time to reflect on their own and discuss as a group. After everyone has shared, ask where the Spirit is guiding this ministry. Based on your discussion, discern your next steps.

NOTES

INTRODUCTION

1. "1971 San Fernando Earthquake," Wikipedia, last updated February 18, 2019, https://tinyurl.com/yxjujj5t.
2. "1971 San Fernando Earthquake," Wikipedia.
3. Some research includes: The National Study of Youth and Religion (Christian Smith, http://youthandreligion.nd.edu/), The Exemplar Youth Ministry Study (Spirit and Culture of Youth Ministry, 2010), Sticky Faith (Kara Powell, Fuller Youth Institute, https://fulleryouthinstitute.org/stickyfaith) and The Confirmation Project (Princeton, https://theconfirmationproject.com/).
4. Kenda Creasy Dean, *Almost Christian: What the Faith of Our Teenagers Is Telling the American Church* (New York: Oxford University Press, 2010).
5. For two examples, see: Clint Schnekloth, *Mediating Faith: Faith Formation in a Trans-media Era* (Minneapolis: Fortress, 2014); and Julie Anne Lytle, *Faith Formation 4.0: Introducing an Ecology of Faith in a Digital Age* (New York: Morehouse, 2013).
6. Clive Thompson, "From Ptolemy to GPS, the Brief History of Maps," *Smithsonian Magazine,* July 2017, https://tinyurl.com/yy2baxct.
7. Rob Eklington et al., *Visionary Leadership in a Turbulent World: Thriving in the New VUCA Context* (Bingley: Emerald Publishing, 2017), 2.

8. Eklington et al., *Visionary Leadership,* 2.

CHAPTER 1: WELCOME TO THE WILDERNESS: EMBRACING THE CALL

1. "A Social Statement on: Our Calling in Education in the ELCA," amended and adopted by the Churchwide Assembly, August 10, 2007, 12.
2. United States Holocaust Memorial Museum, "The German Churches and the Nazi State," Holocaust Encyclopedia, https://tinyurl.com/y5o2s5xp.
3. History, "Westward Expansion," A&E Television Networks, 2019, https://tinyurl.com/8y7wll2.
4. History, "Westward Expansion."
5. Thomas L. Friedman, *Thank You for Being Late: An Optimist's Guide to Thriving in the Age of Accelerations* (New York: Farrar, Straus & Giroux, 2016), 3–5, 15.
6. Eklington et al., *Visionary Leadership*.
7. John H. Westerhoff III, *Will Our Children Have Faith?*, 3rd ed. (New York: Morehouse, 2012), 20.
8. Westerhoff, *Our Children*, 20.
9. Carol Dweck, *Mindset: The New Psychology of Success* (New York: Ballantine, 2016), 65.
10. Dweck, *Mindset*, 27, 58.
11. Kendra Cherry, "What Is a Genius IQ Score?," *verywellmind*, March 11, 2019, http://tinyurl.com/yxos7hsh.
12. Donella Caspersz and Ania Stasinska, "Can We Teach Effective Listening? An Exploratory Study," *Journal of University Teaching & Learning Practice* 12, no. 4 (2015): 1, https://tinyurl.com/y669kp8f.
13. Caspersz and Stasinska, "Effective Listening," 1.
14. Scott Williams, "Listening Effectively," Wright State University–Raj Soin College of Business, accessed July 18, 2018, https://tinyurl.com/y4orna6r.

15. William Ury, "The Power of Listening," filmed November 2014 in San Diego, CA, TED video, 15:40, https://tinyurl.com/y43fqxbu.
16. Caspersz and Stasinska, "Effective Listening," 9.
17. Jack Mezirow et al., *Learning as Transformation: Critical Perspectives on a Theory in Progress* (San Francisco: Jossey-Bass, 2000), 3.
18. Edgar H. Schein, *Humble Inquiry: The Gentle Art of Asking Instead of Telling* (San Francisco: Berrett-Koehler, 2013), 99–100.
19. Mezirow et al., *Learning as Transformation*, 16.
20. Mezirow et al., *Learning as Transformation*, 16.
21. Robert Kegan and Lisa Laskow Lahey, *An Everyone Culture: Becoming a Deliberately Developmental Organization* (Boston: Harvard Business Review Press, 2016), 3.
22. Kegan and Laskow Lahey, *Everyone Culture*, 62–63.
23. Kegan and Laskow Lahey, *Everyone Culture*, 73.
24. Eklington et al., *Visionary Leadership*, 45–46.
25. Eklington et al., *Visionary Leadership*, 45–46.
26. Schein, *Humble Inquiry*, 89–90.
27. Schein, *Humble Inquiry*, 91.

CHAPTER 2: FINDING DYNAMIC STABILITY: GPS FOR THE JOURNEY

1. Schein, *Humble Inquiry*, 7.
2. Mark's version of this story adds that there were wild animals; see Mark 1:13.
3. In John 6, Jesus refers to himself as the bread of life.
4. For more on the reformation, see https://lutheranreformation.org.
5. Martin Luther, "An Introduction to St. Paul's Letter to the Romans," in *Luther's German Bible of 1522*, ed. Johann K. Irmischer, trans. Robert E. Smith, vol. 63 (Erlangen: Hayden & Zimmer, 1854), 124–25.
6. Luther, "St. Paul's," 124–25.
7. David I. Smith, *Learning from the Stranger: Christian Faith and Cultural Diversity* (Grand Rapids: Eerdmans, 2009), 5.

8. Friedman, *Thank You for Being Late*, 198.
9. Friedman, *Thank You for Being Late*, 199.
10. Dave Isay, "Everyone Around You Has a Story the World Needs to Hear," filmed March 2015 in Vancouver, BC, TED video, 21:38, https://tinyurl.com/q8u9.
11. Isay, "Everyone Around You."
12. Isay, "Everyone Around You."
13. StoryCorps, "About StoryCorps," last modified 2019, https://storycorps.org/about/.
14. To see Phil Goldman's work and the interviews, go to https://mzion.org/homz-blog/.
15. StoryCorps, "Great Questions," last modified 2018, https://tinyurl.com/y5dd8585.
16. Dictionary.com, s.v. "dwell," accessed April 22, 2019, https://tinyurl.com/yxjg4dne; *Merriam-Webster Dictionary,* s.v. "dwell," accessed April 22, 2019, https://tinyurl.com/yyj8uuyx.
17. "What Is Lectio Divina?," The Order of Carmelites, https://tinyurl.com/y2qpadpk.
18. Patrick Keifert and Nigel Rooms, *Forming the Missional Church: Creating Deep Cultural Change in Congregations* (Cambridge: Cambridge Grove Books, 2014), 21.
19. Keifert and Rooms, *Missional Church*, 21.
20. Pat Taylor Ellison and Patrick Keifert, *Dwelling in the Word: A Pocket Handbook* (St. Paul: Church Innovations, 2012), 91.

CHAPTER 3: DISCERNING THE TRAIL: ON THE WAY

1. Keifert and Rooms, *Missional Church*, 16.
2. Douglas John Hall, *The End of Christendom and the Future of Christianity* (Eugene, OR: Wipf & Stock, 2002).
3. Douglas John Hall, *The Cross in Our Context: Jesus and the Suffering World* (Minneapolis: Fortress, 2003), 15.
4. Hall, *Cross in Our Context*, 22.
5. Hall, *Cross in Our Context*, 22.
6. Hall, *Cross in Our Context*, 32.

7. Hall, *Cross in Our Context*, 28.
8. Vincent J. Miller, "Taking Consumer Culture Seriously," *Horizons* 27, no. 2 (September 1, 2000): 280.
9. Christian Smith and Melinda Lundquist Denton, *Soul Searching: The Religious and Spiritual Lives of American Teenagers* (New York: Oxford University Press, 2005), 176; italics in original.
10. Smith and Denton, *Soul Searching*, 176.
11. Joyce Mercer, *Welcoming Children: A Practical Theology of Childhood* (St. Louis: Chalice, 2005), 73.
12. Mercer, *Welcoming Children*, 73.
13. Miller, "Taking Consumer Culture Seriously," 283.
14. The *oral* era involved interactions between two or more persons in the same place. In this era, communication was limited by distance and stories were both the medium and the message. In the *written* era communication expanded to include artifacts, like letters, newspapers, and books. In this era, the message and the messenger were separated so messages could be shared across space and time. In the *mass-mediated* era, it became possible to distribute the same message across a wide geographical area to masses of people. The printing press, Morse code, and radio are mediums of mass communication. Our current era is *interactive* communication. Not bound by geography or physical artifacts, communication is broadcastable, portable, instantaneous, and interactive. Mediums include video, phones, and computers. In this era, the message is separated from the messenger and sent through a constellation of devices and platforms. For more, see Lytle, *Faith Formation 4.0*, 51–57.
15. Friedman, *Thank You for Being Late*, 20–21.
16. Clay Shirky, *Here Comes Everyone: The Power of Organizing without Organizations* (New York: Penguin, 2008), 60.
17. Jamie Notter and Maddie Grant, *Humanize: How People-Centric Organizations Succeed in a Social World* (Indianapolis: Que, 2011), 3.
18. Lee Rainie and Barry Wellman, *Networked: The New Social Operating System* (Cambridge: MIT Press, 2012), 6.
19. Rainie and Wellman, *Networked,* 7.

20. Rainie and Wellman, *Networked,* 6.
21. Sherry Turkle, *Alone Together: Why We Expect More from Technology and Less from Each Other* (New York: Basic, 2011), 286.
22. Martin Hilbert, professor at the University of California, Davis, puts it this way: "The digitalization of the world's information stockpile happened in what is a historic blink of an eye: in 1986, less than 1% of the world's mediated information was still stored in digital format. By 2014, less than 0.5% is stored in analog media." Martin Hilbert, "Information Quantity," in *Encyclopedia of Big Data*, ed. Laurie A. Shintler and Connie L. McNeely (Cham: Springer, 2017), https://tinyurl.com/yy228k5j.
23. Jeremy Heimans and Henry Timms, "Understanding 'New Power,'" *Harvard Business Review*, December 2014, https://tinyurl.com/yy8z7oyu.
24. Heimans and Timms, "Understanding 'New Power.'"
25. Notter and Grant, *Humanize*, 28.
26. "The world got flat when all 10 of these flatteners converged around the year 2000. This created a global, Web-enabled playing field that allows for multiple forms of collaboration on research and work in real time, without regard to geography, distance or, in the near future, even language." Thomas Friedman, *The World Is Flat: A Brief History of the Twenty-first Century* (New York: Farrar, Straus & Giroux, 2007), 7.
27. International Networks Archive, "The Magic Bean Shop & The Fries that Bind Us," Princeton, 2003, https://tinyurl.com/l7wpe.
28. Starbucks Corporation, "Company Profile," Starbucks Stories & News, January 24, 2019, https://tinyurl.com/y28dv7hb.
29. International Networks Archive, "Magic Bean."
30. Nayef R. F. Al-Rodhan, "Definitions of Globalization: A Comprehensive Overview and a Proposed Definition," Geneva Centre for Security Policy, June 19, 2006, 6, https://tinyurl.com/yy7d727k.
31. Thomas Friedman, "It's a Flat World, After All," *The New York Times Magazine,* April 3, 2005, https://tinyurl.com/y3pl5w9q.
32. Friedman, *The World Is Flat,* 9–10.
33. Friedman, "It's a Flat World."
34. Quoted in Friedman, *The World Is Flat*, 54.

35. "US Immigration Trends," Migration Policy Institute, https://tinyurl.com/y xzql6f3.
36. Philip Martin, "Trends in Migration to the US," Population Reference Bureau, May 19, 2014, https://tinyurl.com/y5etcc89/.
37. The Pew Charitable Trusts, "Changing Patterns in US Immigration and Population: Immigrants Slow Population Decline in Many Counties," December 2014, https://tinyurl.com/yx9kqm57.
38. US Census, "International Migration Is Projected to Become Primary Driver of US Population Growth for First Time in Nearly Two Centuries," May 15, 2013, https://tinyurl.com/y3g8uu3v.
39. David I. Smith, *Learning from the Stranger: Christian Faith and Cultural Diversity* (Grand Rapids: Eerdmans, 2009), 56.
40. Smith, *Learning from the Stranger,* 56.
41. Smith and Denton, *Soul Searching*, 169.
42. Smith and Denton, *Soul Searching*, 169.
43. Robert D. Putnam and David Campbell, *American Grace: How Religion Divides and Unites Us* (New York: Simon & Schuster, 2010), 4.
44. This study was done prior to Donald Trump's presidency. During his campaign and in his first few years in office, this reality is being tested. Without a change in the public rhetoric, I have a hard time believing this reality will remain true.
45. "American Grace: How Religion Unites and Divides Us," 2016, americangrace.org.
46. "American Grace."
47. Kayla Epstein, "'We Will Rebuild': Pittsburgh's Community Holds Vigil to Mourn—and Unify," *The Washington Post*, October 28, 2018, https://tinyurl.com/y6sw3nk9.
48. Epstein, "We Will Rebuild."
49. Epstein, "We Will Rebuild."
50. MTD has five core tenets: "God exists, who created and orders the world and watches over human life on earth; God wants people to be good, nice, and fair to each other, as taught in the Bible and by most world religions; the central goal in life is to be happy and to feel good about oneself; God does not need to be particularly involved in one's life except when God is needed to resolve a

problem; and good people go to heaven when they die." Smith and Denton, *Soul Searching*, 162–63.

51. Smith and Denton offer a four-level model for understanding religious pluralism in today's North American context. The first level of "Operative American Religion" is *organizational religion*, or formal religion expressed in institutions, denominations, religious organizations, and established congregations. This level is the one most think of when referring to religion. *Individual religion* is a level below, representing people's lived faith. This level is "eclectic, idiosyncratic, and syncretistic" (168), mixing various, often contradictory, practices and beliefs. *American civil religion* is the level above organizational religion and, as noted above, represents an overarching national posture. *Moralistic Therapeutic Deism,* a fourth level that falls above individual religion and below organizational religion, is a new operating framework that describes the findings of the National Study of Youth and Religion. Adapted from Smith and Denton, *Soul Searching*, 162–71.
52. Smith and Denton, *Soul Searching*, 169.
53. Paul Hiebert, "Conversion, Culture and Cognitive Categories," *Gospel in Context* 11, no. 4 (October 1978): 24–29.
54. "About CBS," The Center for Barth Studies at Princeton Theological Seminary, https://tinyurl.com/yy2xbmvm.
55. "You shall not oppress a stranger; you know the heart of a stranger, for you were strangers in the land of Egypt" (Exodus 23:9 RSV).
56. "But no stranger had to spend the night in the street, for my door was always open to the traveler" (Job 31:32 NIV).

CHAPTER 4: PEOPLE ON THE MOVE: #LIVINGABUNDANT

1. David Brooks in his column in the *New York Times*, June 21, 2016; quoted in Friedman, *Thank You for Being Late*, 426.
2. REI Staff, "The History of #OptOutside," REI, October 29, 2017, https://tinyurl.com/yxduxoj3.
3. Jerry Stritzke, "Making the Case for Life Outside," REI, October 19, 2018, https://tinyurl.com/y45yay8s

4. "Not a jog around the block, a ride on a bike, or a night in a tent." Stritzke, "Making the Case for Life Outside."
5. REI Staff, "The Path Ahead," REI, October 2017, https://tinyurl.com/y5zqhtec.
6. In Genesis 1, God created the heavens and the earth, and in Revelation 21, God eliminates death.
7. New Testament scholar Craig Koester says, "Resurrection is the promise of a new existence, a transformed existence." Craig R. Koester, "Commentary on Revelation 21:1–6a," *Working Preacher,* Luther Seminary, November 1, 2009, https://tinyurl.com/y4nf2cna.
8. Evangelical Lutheran Church in America, *Evangelical Lutheran Worship* (Minneapolis: Augsburg Fortress, 2006), 236.
9. Revelation 21 draws from Ezekiel 37:27 and Isaiah 25:7–8, 43:18–19, 61:10, and 65:17–18. See also Koester, "Commentary on Revelation 21:1–6a."
10. Koester, "Commentary on Revelation 21:1–6a."
11. C. Otto Scharmer, *The Essentials of Theory U: Core Principles and Application* (Oakland: Berrett-Koehler, 2018).
12. C. Otto Scharmer, *Learning from the Emerging Future* (San Francisco: Berrett-Koehler, 2013), 3; italics in original.
13. Chip Heath and Dan Heath, *Switch: How to Change Things When Change Is Hard* (New York: Broadway Books, 2010).
14. Scharmer, *Essentials of Theory U*, 10.
15. Scharmer, *Essentials of Theory U*, 133.
16. Andrew Zirschky, *Beyond the Screen: Youth Ministry for the Connected but Alone Generation* (Nashville: Abingdon, 2015), 120. On page 121, Zirschky says, "The self in networked culture is thus a production."
17. Friedman, *Thanks for Being Late*, 6.
18. John Zizioulas, *Being as Communion: Studies in Personhood and the Church* (Crestwood, NY: St. Vladimir's Seminary Press, 1985), 49.
19. Zirschky, *Beyond the Screen*, 124.
20. According to Jürgen Moltmann, "An 'individual' is an anonymous being, without name and family. A 'person' is, by contrast,

a human being in the resonance-field of his or her relationships of I-you-we or I-myself or I-it. . . . Within this network of relationships the human subject becomes a subject of giving and taking, hearing and responding, touching and experiencing. Modern individualism does not serve the freedom of human persons, but more their new enslavement." Jürgen Moltmann, "An Old Magic for a New Trinitarian Theology," in *Trinity, Community, and Power: Mapping Trajectories in Wesleyan Theology*, ed. M. Douglas Meeks (Nashville: Kingswood, 2000), 124.

21. Robert D. Putnam and Lewis M. Feldstein, *Better Together: Restoring the American Community* (New York: Simon & Schuster, 2003), 2.
22. Putnam and Feldstein, *Better Together*, 294.
23. Zirschky, *Beyond the Screen*, 148.
24. Zirschky, *Beyond the Screen*, 57.
25. Zirschky, *Beyond the Screen*, 54.
26. Friedman, *Thank You for Being Late*, 6.
27. Putnam and Feldstein, *Better Together*, 294.
28. Zirschky, *Beyond the Screen*, 52.
29. Smith, *Learning from the Stranger*, 5.
30. Smith, *Learning from the Stranger*, 54.
31. David Livermore, *Cultural Intelligence: Improving Your CQ to Engage Our Multicultural World* (Grand Rapids: Baker, 2009), 55.
32. Livermore, *Cultural Intelligence,* 15.
33. Livermore, *Cultural Intelligence,* 15.
34. Shirky, *Here Comes Everyone*, 20–21.
35. Kegan and Laskow Lahey, *An Everyone Culture*, 5.
36. Kegan and Laskow Lahey, *An Everyone Culture*, 86.
37. Cathy Lynn Grossman, "'Out of Many Faiths,' Eboo Patel Sees a Potluck, Not a Melting Pot Nation," *Publishers Weekly*, July 25, 2018, https://tinyurl.com/y6olrho2.
38. Grossman, "'Out of Many Faiths.'"
39. Grossman, "'Out of Many Faiths.'"
40. Yonat Shimron, "From 'Judeo-Christian' to 'Potluck Nation,' Eboo Patel Pleads for Religious Pluralism," Religion News Service, August 30, 2018, https://tinyurl.com/y46uoolc.

41. Moltmann, "An Old Magic," 125.
42. This points to Leviticus 19:18 and Deuteronomy 6:5.
43. Smith, *Learning from the Stranger*, 60.
44. A neighbor (within Leviticus 19:18) would have been "a fellow member of the covenant community" (Smith, *Learning from the Stranger*, 62) or (within Leviticus 19:34) a vulnerable foreigner or immigrant. Audrey West, "Commentary on Luke 10:25–42," *Working Preacher*, Luther Seminary, March 5, 2017, https://tinyurl.com/y5qum5na.
45. Smith, *Learning from the Stranger*, 63.
46. Joe Corpora, "Road to Jericho (Setting for the Good Samaritan)," *FaithND*, University of Notre Dame, https://tinyurl.com/y5257vdq.
47. Smith, *Learning from the Stranger*, 65–66.
48. Smith, *Learning from the Stranger*, 69.
49. Smith, *Learning from the Stranger*, 74.
50. Roger Federer, "Roger Federer: Quarter-final," press conference, July 12, 2018, https://tinyurl.com/yy65fr2y.
51. Federer, "Roger Federer: Quarter-final."
52. James H. Evans, *Playing: Christian Explorations of Daily Living* (Minneapolis: Fortress, 2010), 11.
53. Charles Graeber, "Meet the Carousing, Harmonica-Playing Texan Who Just Won a Nobel for His Cancer Breakthrough," *Wired*, October 22, 2018, https://tinyurl.com/y67jy3c9.
54. Graeber, "Harmonica-Playing Texan."
55. Lesslie Newbigin, *The Open Secret: Introduction to the Theology of Mission* (Grand Rapids: Eerdmans, 1978), 69.
56. Kathleen A. Cahalan, *The Stories We Live: Finding God's Calling All Around Us* (Grand Rapids: Eerdmans, 2017), xi–xii.
57. Cahalan, *The Stories We Live,* xi–xii.
58. Cahalan, *The Stories We Live*, xii; italics in original.

CHAPTER 5: TRAVELERS GATHERING AND SCATTERING: SANCTUARIES, CAMPFIRES, AND OUTPOSTS

1. Friedman, *Thank You for Being Late*, 452–53.

2. Jars of Clay, "This Road," Essential Records, 2000.
3. Hall, *Cross in Our Context*, 31.
4. Hall, *Cross in Our Context*, 24.
5. Miller, "Taking Consumer Culture Seriously," 277.
6. Derek Sivers, "How to Start a Movement," filmed February 2010 in Long Beach, CA, TED video, 2:55, https://tinyurl.com/yyytkc9h.
7. Jay Pathak and Dave Runyon, *The Art of Neighboring: Building Genuine Relationships Right Outside Your Door* (Grand Rapids: Baker, 2012), 19.
8. Pathak and Runyon, *The Art of Neighboring,* 19.
9. Pathak and Runyon, *The Art of Neighboring,* 23–24.
10. Pathak and Runyon, *The Art of Neighboring,* 25.
11. Pathak and Runyon, *The Art of Neighboring,* 36–37.
12. Pathak and Runyon, *The Art of Neighboring,* 39.
13. Dave Runyon and Jay Pathak, "About," The Art of Neighboring, https://www.artofneighboring.com/about/.
14. Pathak and Runyon, *The Art of Neighboring*, 173.
15. Robert Muthiah, *The Sabbath Experiment: Spiritual Formation for Living in a Non-Stop World* (Eugene, OR: Cascade, 2015), 12.
16. Muthiah, *The Sabbath Experiment,* 100–102.
17. Muthiah, *The Sabbath Experiment,* 9–10.
18. Angela Reed, Richard Osmer, and Marcus Smucker, *Spiritual Companionship: A Guide to Protestant Theology and Practice* (Grand Rapids: Baker Academic, 2015), 36–37.
19. Reed, Osmer, and Smucker, *Spiritual Companionship*, xx.
20. Reed, Osmer, and Smucker, *Spiritual Companionship*, xiv.

BIBLIOGRAPHY

Al-Rodhan, Nayef R. F. "Definitions of Globalization: A Comprehensive Overview and a Proposed Definition." Geneva Centre for Security Policy, June 19, 2006. https://tinyurl.com/yy7d727k.

Baab, Lynne M. *The Power of Listening: Building Skills for Mission and Ministry*. Lanham: Rowman & Littlefield, 2014.

Braaten, Carl E. *Principles of Lutheran Theology*, 2nd edition. Minneapolis: Fortress, 2007.

Cahalan, Kathleen A. *The Stories We Live: Finding God's Calling All Around Us*. Grand Rapids: Eerdmans, 2017.

Caspersz, Donella, and Ania Stasinska. "Can We Teach Effective Listening? An Exploratory Study." *Journal of University Teaching & Learning Practice* 12, no. 4 (2015). https://tinyurl.com/y669kp8f.

Center for Barth Studies at Princeton Theological Seminary. "About CBS." https://tinyurl.com/yy2xbmvm.

Cherry, Kendra. "What Is a Genius IQ Score?" *verywellmind*, March 11, 2019. https://tinyurl.com/yxos7hsh.

Corpora, Joe. "Road to Jericho (Setting for the Good Samaritan)." *FaithND*, University of Notre Dame. https://tinyurl.com/y5257vdq.

Dean, Kenda Creasy. *Almost Christian: What the Faith of Our Teenagers Is Telling the American Church*. New York: Oxford University Press, 2010.

Dolan, Marian. "Transformative Listening." Filmed February 2015 at Coconut Grove, FL. TED video, 19:48. https://youtu.be/e1ZxIFKddNQ.

Dweck, Carol. *Mindset: The New Psychology of Success*. New York: Ballantine, 2016.

Eklington, Rob, Madeleine van der Steege, Judith Glick-Smith, and Jennifer Moss Breen, eds. *Visionary Leadership in a Turbulent World: Thriving in the New VUCA Context*. Bingley: Emerald Publishing, 2017.

Ellison, Pat Taylor, and Patrick Keifert. *Dwelling in the Word: A Pocket Handbook*. St. Paul: Church Innovations, 2012.

Epstein, Kayla. "'We Will Rebuild': Pittsburgh's Community Holds Vigil to Mourn—and Unify." *The Washington Post*, October 28, 2018. https://tinyurl.com/y6sw3nk9.

Evangelical Lutheran Church in America. *Evangelical Lutheran Worship*. Minneapolis: Augsburg Fortress, 2006.

Evans, James H. *Playing: Christian Explorations of Daily Living*. Minneapolis: Fortress, 2010.

Federer, Roger. "Roger Federer: Quarter-final." Press conference, July 12, 2018. https://tinyurl.com/yy65fr2y.

Friedman, Thomas. "It's a Flat World, After All." *The New York Times Magazine*, April 3, 2005. https://tinyurl.com/y3pl5w9q.

———. *Thank You for Being Late: An Optimist's Guide to Thriving in the Age of Accelerations*. New York: Farrar, Straus & Giroux, 2016.

———. *The World Is Flat: A Brief History of the Twenty-first Century*. New York: Farrar, Straus & Giroux, 2007.

Graeber, Charles. "Meet the Carousing, Harmonica-Playing Texan Who Just Won a Nobel for His Cancer Breakthrough." *Wired*, October 22, 2018. https://tinyurl.com/y67jy3c9.

Grossman, Cathy L. "'Out of Many Faiths,' Eboo Patel Sees a Potluck, Not a Melting Pot Nation." *Publishers Weekly*, July 25, 2018. https://tinyurl.com/y6olrho2.

Guder, Darrell. *Missional Church: A Vision for the Sending of the Church in North America*. Grand Rapids: Eerdmans, 1998.

Hall, Douglas John. *The Cross in Our Context: Jesus and the Suffering World*. Minneapolis: Fortress, 2003.

———. *The End of Christendom and the Future of Christianity*. Eugene, OR: Wipf & Stock, 2002.

Heath, Chip, and Dan Heath. *Switch: How to Change Things When Change Is Hard*. New York: Broadway Books, 2010.

Heimans, Jeremy, and Henry Timms. "Understanding 'New Power," *Harvard Business Review*. December 2014, https://tinyurl.com/yy8z7oyu.

Hiebert, Paul. "Conversion, Culture and Cognitive Categories." *Gospel in Context* 11, no. 4 (October 1978): 24–29.

Hilbert, Martin. "Information Quantity." In *Encyclopedia of Big Data* Edited by Laurie A. Shintler and Connie L. McNeely. Cham: Springer, 2017. https://tinyurl.com/yy228k5j.

History. "Westward Expansion." A&E Television Networks, 2019. https://tinyurl.com/8y7wll2.

Hoffman, Paul. *Faith Forming Faith: Bringing New Christians to Baptism and Beyond*. Eugene, OR: Cascade, 2012.

Holocaust Encyclopedia. "The German Churches and the Nazi State." https ://tinyurl.com/y5o2s5xp.

International Networks Archive. "The Magic Bean Shop & the Fries That Bind Us." Princeton, 2003. https://tinyurl.com/l7wpe.

Isay, Dave. "Everyone Around You Has a Story the World Needs to Hear." Filmed March 2015 in Vancouver, BC. TED video, 21:38. https://tinyurl.com/q8u9.

———. *Listening Is an Act of Love*. New York: Penguin, 2007.

Kegan, Robert, and Lisa Laskow Lahey. *An Everyone Culture: Becoming a Deliberately Developmental Organization*. Boston: Harvard Business Review Press, 2016.

Keifert, Patrick. *We Are Here Now: A New Missional Age*. Eagle: Allehon, 2006.

Keifert, Patrick, and Nigel Rooms. *Forming the Missional Church: Creating Deep Cultural Change in Congregations*. Cambridge: Cambridge Grove Books, 2014.

Koester, Craig R. "Commentary on Revelation 21:1–6a." *Working Preacher,* Luther Seminary, November 1, 2009. https://tinyurl.com/y4nf2cna.

Livermore, David. *Cultural Intelligence: Improving Your CQ to Engage Our Multicultural World*. Grand Rapids: Baker, 2009.

Luther, Martin. "An Introduction to St. Paul's Letter to the Romans." In *Luther's German Bible of 1522*. Edited by Johann K. Irmischer. Translated by Robert E. Smith. Vol. 63. Erlangen: Hayden & Zimmer, 1854.

Lytle, Julie Anne. *Faith Formation 4.0: Introducing an Ecology of Faith in a Digital Age*. New York: Morehouse, 2013.

Martin, Philip. "Trends in Migration to the US." Population Reference Bureau, May 19, 2014. https://tinyurl.com/y5etcc89.

Mercer, Joyce. *Welcoming Children: A Practical Theology of Childhood*. St. Louis: Chalice, 2005.

Mezirow, Jack. *Learning as Transformation: Critical Perspectives on a Theory in Progress*. San Francisco: Jossey-Bass, 2000.

Migration Policy Institute. "US Immigration Trends." https://tinyurl.com/yxzql6f3.

Miller, Vincent J. "Taking Consumer Culture Seriously." *Horizons* 27, no. 2 (September 1, 2000): 276–95.

Moltmann, Jürgen. "An Old Magic for a New Trinitarian Theology." *Trinity, Community, and Power: Mapping Trajectories in Wesleyan Theology*. Edited by M. Douglas Meeks. Nashville: Kingswood, 2000.

Muthiah, Robert. *The Sabbath Experiment: Spiritual Formation for Living in a Non-Stop World*. Eugene, OR: Cascade, 2015.

Newbigin, Lesslie. *The Open Secret: Introduction to the Theology of Mission* (Grand Rapids: Eerdmans, 1978), 69.

Notter, Jamie, and Maddie Grant. *Humanize: How People-Centric Organizations Succeed in a Social World.* Indianapolis: Que, 2011.

Pathak, Jay, and Dave Runyon. *The Art of Neighboring: Building Genuine Relationships Right Outside Your Door.* Grand Rapids: Baker, 2012.

Pew Charitable Trusts. "Changing Patterns in US Immigration and Population: Immigrants Slow Population Decline in Many Counties." December 2014. https://tinyurl.com/yx9kqm57.

Putnam, Robert D., and David Campbell. *American Grace: How Religion Divides and Unites Us.* New York: Simon & Schuster, 2010.

Putnam, Robert D., and Lewis M. Feldstein. *Better Together: Restoring the American Community.* New York: Simon & Schuster, 2003.

Rainie, Lee, and Barry Wellman. *Networked: The New Social Operating System.* Cambridge: MIT Press, 2012.

Reed, Angela, Richard Osmer, and Marcus Smucker. *Spiritual Companionship: A Guide to Protestant Theology and Practice.* Grand Rapids: Baker Academic, 2015.

REI Staff. "The History of #OptOutside." Recreational Equipment, October 29, 2017. https://tinyurl.com/.yxduxoj3.

———. "The Path Ahead." Recreational Equipment, October 2017, https://tinyurl.com/y5zqhtec.

Scharmer, C. Otto. "The Ego to Eco Framework." Filmed April 2017 for Presencing Institute in Cambridge, MA. Video, 2:51. https://tinyurl.com/y52k2joh.

———. *The Essentials of Theory U: Core Principles and Application*. Oakland: Berrett-Koehler, 2018.

———. *Learning from the Emerging Future*. San Francisco: Berrett-Koehler, 2013.

Schein, Edgar H. *Humble Inquiry: The Gentle Art of Asking Instead of Telling*. San Francisco: Berrett-Koehler, 2013.

Schnekloth, Clint. *Mediating Faith: Faith Formation in a Transmedia Era*. Minneapolis: Fortress, 2014.

Shimron, Yonat. "From 'Judeo-Christian' to 'Potluck Nation,' Eboo Patel Pleads for Religious Pluralism." Religion News Service, August 30, 2018. https://tinyurl.com/y46uoolc.

Shirky, Clay. *Here Comes Everyone: The Power of Organizing without Organizations*. New York: Penguin, 2008.

Sivers, Derek. "How to Start a Movement." Filmed February 2010 in Long Beach, CA, TED video, 2:55, https://tinyurl.com/yyytkc9h.

Smith, Christian, and Melinda Lundquist Denton. *Soul Searching: The Religious and Spiritual Lives of American Teenagers*. New York: Oxford University Press, 2005.

Smith, David I. *Learning from the Stranger: Christian Faith and Cultural Diversity*. Grand Rapids: Eerdmans, 2009.

Starbucks Corporation. "Company Profile." Starbucks Stories & News January 24, 2019, https ://tinyurl.com/y3qspeg9.

StoryCorps. "About StoryCorps." Last modified 2019. https://storycorps.org/about/.

———. "Great Questions." Last modified 2018. https://tinyurl.com/y5dd8585.

Stritzke, Jerry. "Making the Case for Life Outside." Recreational Equipment, October 19, 2018. https://tinyurl.com/y45yay8s

Tanner, Kathryn. *Theories of Culture: A New Agenda for Theology*. Minneapolis: Fortress Press, 1997.

Thompson, Clive. "From Ptolemy to GPS, the Brief History of Maps," *Smithsonian Magazine*, July 2017. https://tinyurl.com/yy2baxct.

Turkle, Sherry. *Alone Together: Why We Expect More from Technology and Less from Each Other*. New York: Basic, 2011.

Ury, William. "The Power of Listening." Filmed November 2014 at San Diego, CA. TED video, 15:40. https://tinyurl.com/y43fqxbu.

US Census. "International Migration Is Projected to Become Primary Driver of US Population Growth for First Time in Nearly Two Centuries." May 15, 2013. https://tinyurl.com/y3g8uu3v.

West, Audrey. "Commentary on Luke 10:25–42." *Working Preacher*, Luther Seminary, March 5, 2017. https://tinyurl.com/y5qum5na.

Westerhoff, John H., III, *Will Our Children Have Faith?* 3rd ed. New York: Morehouse, 2012.

Williams, Scott. "Listening Effectively." Wright State University–Raj Soin College of Business, accessed July 18, 2018. https://tinyurl.com/y4orna6r.

Zirschky, Andrew. *Beyond the Screen: Youth Ministry for the Connected but Alone Generation*. Nashville: Abingdon, 2015.

Zizioulas, John. *Being as Communion: Studies in Personhood and the Church*. Crestwood, NY: St. Vladimir's Seminary Press, 1985.

ACKNOWLEDGMENTS

The gestation period of a book is hard to calculate. For me, the quest to form faith in dialog with contextual realities was birthed thirty years ago. Along the way, many people and communities have been critical conversation partners as they allowed me to ask hard questions, experiment with new approaches, and trust in God's guidance. I am particularly thankful for Prince of Peace Lutheran Church in Burnsville, Minnesota; the ELCA Youth Ministry Network; the Confirmation Project team; and my colleagues and students at Luther Seminary. I learn best by tackling real-life challenges within communities of learning with diverse people and ideas. I am grateful for the fertile ground you provided me to develop these ideas.

I am indebted to teachers and colleagues who have accompanied me in cultivating a theology that integrates our lived experiences with our understanding of God. Curiosity and questions directed me to an academic conversation I longed for but did not know existed. Centered on congregations, missiology, and leadership, I found a home and developed a missional understanding of church within a Lutheran key. Craig Van Gelder,

Patrick Keifert, Alvin Luedke, Mary Hess, Kristine Stache, Mary Sue Drier, Dwight Zscheile, Dan Anderson, Kyle Small, Michael Binder, and Steve Thomason are just some of the thought partners who have challenged and encouraged me. Thank you for being my colleagues and co-creators of the future.

This project was possible because of a sabbatical. Having time and space to read, study, write, and think was a gift. Thank you to Luther Seminary, in particular the Board of Trustees and my colleagues, for making this possible. My hope is that the investment you made in me witnesses to the gospel in such a way that future generations know God's love.

Many people offered tangible support. Thank you to my reading team, who read drafts of this work in process. You form faith on a daily basis, and your input refined this book and supported me as I translated my ideas into a resource for congregations. Thank you, Pastor Perry Aalgaard, Rachel Alley, Mark Jackson, Pastor Jessica McEvers, Per Nestigen, Pastor Jen Quanbeck, and Charlie Roberts. Thank you also to Catherine Anderson, Dawn Trautman, and Vicki Haugo for being conversation partners and providing spaces for me to think and write.

My Christian formation was influenced by many vibrant communities. Salem Lutheran Church in Glendale, California; Hope Lutheran Church in Fargo, North Dakota; and Christ the King Lutheran in New Brighton, Minnesota, all left their mark on my journey of faith growing up. For fifty years, my family has made faith part of our ordinary activities. You, more than any other community, have helped me integrate faith into my way of life. My grandparents were witnesses to faithfulness as they navigated the wilderness terrain of their time. My parents extended grace and love in a way that allowed me to discover my own path. My siblings and their families kept life real. My husband and our daughters live this amazing journey with me. Thank you for allowing my questions to become learning moments that awakened an explorer's mindset. My becoming journey is not over.

A special thanks to my husband and our girls. Eric, Jordan, and Elizabeth, your love anchors my world and allows me to experience God's overflowing love every day. You help me see the expansiveness of God's love and God's promised future in ways I could never have imagined. I live abundantly with you in my life. The future is unknown, but I receive glimpses of what is emerging as we accompany each other in discovering a Christian way of life together. Love you!

WORD & WORLD BOOKS

THEOLOGY FOR CHRISTIAN MINISTRY

Informing and inspiring Christian leaders and communities to proclaim God's *Word* to a *World* God created and loves. Articulating the fullness of both realities and the creative intersection between them.

Word & World Books is a partnership between Luther Seminary, the board of the periodical *Word & World*, and Fortress Press.

Books in the series include:

Future Faith: Ten Challenges Reshaping Christianity in the 21st Century by Wesley Granberg Michaelson (2018)

Liberating Youth from Adolescence by Jeremy P. Myers (2018)

Elders Rising: The Promise and Peril of Aging by Roland Martinson (2018)

I Can Do No Other: The Church's New Here We Stand Moment by Anna M. Madsen (2019)

Intercultural Church: A Biblical Vision for an Age of Migration by Safwat Marzouk (2019)

Rooted and Renewing: Imagining the Church's Future in Light of Its New Testament Origins by Troy M. Troftgruben (2019)
Journeying in the Wilderness: Forming Faith in the 21st Century by Terri Martinson Elton (2020)